The Student's Guide to Preparing Dissertations and Theses

2nd Edition

Brian Allison and Phil Race

RoutledgeFalmer
Taylor & Francis Group

LONDON AND NEW YORK

First edition published in 1997
by Kogan Page Limited
120 Pentonville Road
London N1 9JN

This edition published in 2004
by RoutledgeFalmer
2 Park Square, Milton Park, Oxon, OX14 4RN

Simultaneously published in the USA and Canada
by RoutledgeFalmer
270 Madison Ave, New York, NY 10016

Reprinted in 2004

RoutledgeFalmer is an imprint of the Taylor & Francis Group

© 1997 Brian Allison
© 2004 Brian Allison and Phil Race

Typeset in Goudy and Gill by BC Typesetting Ltd, Bristol
Printed and bound in Great Britain by
MPG Books, Bodmin, Cornwall

British Library Cataloguing in Publication Data
A catalogue record for this book is available from the British Library

Library of Congress Cataloging in Publication Data
A catalog record for this book has been requested

ISBN 0–415–33486–1

Contents

Figures

Foreword to this edition

This new edition of *The Student's Guide to Preparing Dissertations and Theses* is firmly based on its predecessor published by Brian Allison in 1997. In updating and revising this edition, I have tried to retain as much as possible of the wisdom and expertise which the late Professor Allison brought to his original work.

However, in the years since the last edition was published, a number of things have changed, not least the fact that most dissertations and theses nowadays are word processed rather than typed, and there have been significant changes in the expected style and layout of dissertations and theses, reflected by the local practices and regulations of individual universities and colleges.

In the present edition, I have added some brief new sections about the *processes* involved in putting together a dissertation and thesis, and preparing for what usually follows – a viva or oral exam.

Professor Allison took great care to explain many details about putting together dissertations, in particular about how to cite other people's work in your own writing, and how to compile a bibliography carefully and precisely. Rather than simply repeat the examples he chose to use (many of which are by now quite dated), I have chosen to invent new fictitious references and quotations to illustrate *how* to go about the task.

At the time of writing, many things are continuing to change. For example, it used to be the case that headings, titles and some other elements of a dissertation were expected to be presented in upper-case lettering when typed, but with the use of word processing allowing a variety of print sizes, and **bold** as well as normal print, the local practice in many institutions has continued to evolve towards a more readable style for such things, using lower case rather than capital letters (indeed the use of upper case is nowadays often frowned on for

anything more than a few words at a time, and is referred to as 'shout-
ing' in electronic communication and web design).

This means that you are well advised to look carefully at recent local
practice in your own institution when making decisions about how
exactly you are going to lay out your own dissertation or thesis, choosing examples of work which turned out to be successful, of course.

I hope that the changes and additions I have made to this book will
prove useful to readers, and will help to extend the valuable work of
Brian Allison, underpinning it all.

Phil Race
July 2003

Preface

This book is written for students following courses in which a dissertation or thesis is an important part of the course or examination requirements. It is applicable to most subject fields in different institutions and countries. Apart from being designed to help students in what is invariably a hurried and tense part of their studies, it is also intended to relieve course tutors and research supervisors from having to respond to endless questions about what are often little more than very routine matters.

Although of different origins, the terms 'dissertation' and 'thesis' have come to be used synonymously and they are used as such in this guide. The material here is based on an earlier publication which was revised a number of times to ensure that it answered the kinds of questions students raise about the formalities of dissertation or thesis preparation. Students' comments and queries, therefore, contributed a great deal to the form and content. Advice and comments from colleagues have also been most helpful in developing this book.

The requirements for the presentation of dissertations and theses are often specified in the assessment regulations of individual universities and colleges, but such regulations tend to focus on the expected numbers of words and the procedures for submission, rather than the form of the dissertations or theses. The procedures laid out here are likely to fulfil the expectations for dissertation presentation in most institutions.

Other developments have taken place in recent years which affect the production of dissertations and theses as well as other forms of research reports. These include the increased access to computer technology, particularly word-processors, database programmes and desktop publishing facilities, as well as the increased availability of photocopying and other means of graphic reproduction. Similarly, the increased accessibility of reference material in non-book media, notably through the Internet has had to be accommodated within the system of bibliographical referencing.

With advances in multimedia technology, there is the possibility of students in some institutions being able to submit dissertations or research reports in other than paper formats, such as on CD-ROM. While it is beyond the brief of this book to lay out how the technological aspects of such materials should be managed and presented, it can be taken that the structure of the research report and the presentation of the text-based material included in the presentation should follow broadly the procedures described here.

A further development has been the formulation of examination regulations that permit the main body of material submitted for assessment to be in some form of practical work, such as may be presented in an exhibition. In such cases, the procedures laid down in this guide should be followed not only for the submission of any substantive documentation required to accompany the work but also for any literal documentation, such as labelling or textual explanations, supporting the practical work submitted. It is normally required that submissions of this kind include a permanent record of the work, such as in the form of photographs, video tapes or DVDs, submitted with, or as part of, the dissertation. In this case, the procedures laid down in the present book for the inclusion of appendices may be used as a starting point.

This book is intended to be used as a working document and, as far as possible, the layout of the text itself has been presented as an example for dissertation presentation, though of course the page size of this book is quite different from the A4 size used for dissertations. This guide may also be of use to course tutors as well as research supervisors and examiners, by providing to some extent a model against which dissertation presentation may be assessed.

In updating the content of this book for the present edition, the fact that most dissertations are now word-processed rather than 'typed' has been addressed. This means that many more research students now do most of the preparation of successive drafts themselves, even though many continue to have their work brought into its final form by a professional typist.

Brian Allison, 1996
with minor changes by Phil Race, 2003

Introduction

A dissertation or thesis is a research report. This guide is designed to help students, and others who are inexperienced in preparing a dissertation or thesis, to overcome some of the main problems of format and style that frequently occur. A dissertation or thesis is, however, only a medium through which research is reported and, of course, the research itself is the most important consideration. No matter how well a research report is presented, the value of the report will be dependent upon the quality of the research that is being reported.

That said, the quality of the final printed version of a dissertation remains important, not least the degree to which it conforms to the expected standards of layout and production for dissertations in the institution awarding the research degree concerned. Even if the content of a dissertation is exemplary, it can still be let down by non-compliance with the sometimes quite 'fussy' rules and regulations concerning layout and format. It is then tiresome and time-consuming to have to re-submit a final version of the dissertation after the content itself has been 'passed'.

A great deal of support is already available to help both the novice and experienced researcher to acquire knowledge and experience in the ways research can be carried out. Most of the research carried out in the natural and social sciences assumes a 'positivistic' stance. Positivistic research subscribes to the 'scientific method', which proceeds from the identification of a problem to the analysis of the problem, the formulation of hypotheses and the testing of those hypotheses, initially by deduction and subsequently by action.

An alternative approach, developed particularly, but not exclusively, within the social sciences, is the 'phenomenological' or 'naturalistic' approach, which assumes any situation to be unique. Naturalistic research does not subscribe to the 'scientific method' and is characterised most often by description that cannot be generalised.

The variety of methods through which research can be pursued generally fall into a number of main categories:

- comparative research;
- descriptive research;
- experimental research;
- historical research;
- naturalistic research;
- philosophical research;
- practical research.

The particular procedures and strategies implicit in all of these methods have been developed through practice over long periods of time. Clearly, the kind of research question being asked determines the principal method through which it can be answered and, reciprocally, a particular research method being used prescribes the kind of question for which an answer may be sought. In practice, although a particular research problem may be pursued through one of the principal research methods, it is likely that aspects of the project will require more than one method to be employed. For example, most social science surveys using descriptive research methods require an historical enquiry into the circumstances leading to the situation being surveyed and a philosophical analysis of the issues being investigated.

The established procedures for these various methods provide indispensable frameworks to guide students in the ways of formulating research questions, developing relevant research designs, selecting appropriate enquiry methods, choosing or devising research instruments and tools and deciding upon ways of analysing data.

The contexts of research

In addition to the acquisition of research skills and the practice of various research methods, there are two matters of considerable importance: the selection of a research topic in the first place and knowing about the various forms in which research is reported.

Sources of research topics

Any research project begins with a topic, which may be in the form of a question being asked, a problem that needs to be solved, or a field which needs to be reviewed. As the research topic is of primary importance, one of the biggest dilemmas for would-be researchers is what to research into or, in other words, where to find a research topic. Finding a worthwhile topic is not easy, particularly as identifying a previously unexamined question invariably requires a comprehensive understanding of the subject field, which few students are likely to have. However, finding a topic need not be overly stressful if the task is undertaken systematically and with common sense. In general, there are five main sources for research topics and these apply to all disciplines:

- the 'felt need' to address an identified problem or question;
- the existing literature of the subject field;
- the deeper knowledge of a field held by research supervisors;
- the thrust of institutional research in a particular university or college;
- commissioned or sponsored research.

It is very important to note that any of the five sources described may be used to identify a topic for research, and indeed that these sources often overlap. They are all valid sources and one is not more important than, or preferable to, any of the others.

The 'felt need' to address an identified problem or question

A topic from this source originates with the researcher who identifies a problem as a consequence of experience in, and some considerable knowledge of, the field. This quite often comes from an observed discrepancy or a nagging feeling that something is 'wrong' or problematic with the status quo in a discipline. This feeling might arise, for example, because of some unusual or otherwise unaccountable behaviour in a technical or chemical process, or from an observation of the way some people behave for which there is no ready explanation. Examples of the former might be Isaac Newton's enquiries into gravity, which followed his wonderment at why the apple falling on his head hit him with a particular amount of force, or Archimedes' research into the measurement of the volume of irregular solids, following his observation of the rise in the water level as he climbed into the bath. Examples of the latter might come from a teacher's observation that more male than female students opt for technology or computer science courses, or an art gallery curator's observation that the number of people in the gallery varies with the time of day.

The existing literature of the subject field

The literature of the subject field is an important source of research topics. The text books and research journals for any subject describes what is already known about the subject and, therefore, can also indicate the gaps in knowledge. Quite often there are conflicting theories or there may be disagreement about how particular phenomena can be explained. An example of conflicting theories from the field of psychology relates to why children draw the way they do: there is the theory that 'Children draw what they know' which appears to be diametrically opposed to the other theory that 'Children draw what they see'. This apparent conflict could be worthy of research. Research reports – whether they are reports submitted for academic qualifications as dissertations or theses, or reports published by professional research organisations – are a vital part of the literature of any field. Summary research reports or abstracts are regularly published in a broad range of research journals such as *Nature, Chemical Abstracts* or *Studies in Art Education*. Research reports in the form of dissertations or theses submitted by students for MA, MSc, MPhil and PhD research degrees are normally held by the library of the university or college.

Almost every research report includes a section with a heading something like 'Possibilities for future research'. This section of a research report often refers to questions that arose during the research project but were unanswered either because they were outside the scope of the project or because there was insufficient time to pursue them. Building upon previous research and following up questions raised in earlier researches is one of the most important sources of professional research activity.

A good grasp of the kinds of research topic pursued in a subject can be gained by carrying out searches of specialist subject research indexes. Research indexes, which may be in book form or databases accessed using computers, are normally held in the library, as described later in this guide. It is worth looking at the titles of completed research reports listed in the indexes to see how they have been formulated. Some titles are very precisely formulated whereas others are vague. With familiarity with the subject, it might be possible to identify from the indexes those areas or topics that have been well researched, and those that have been minimally researched. It may even be possible to infer topics that have yet to be studied.

The deeper knowledge of a field held by research supervisors

All student research is guided by members of staff acting as research supervisors. Some departments in universities and higher education colleges have appointed readers or professors, and these posts often indicate a departmental responsibility for research, which usually includes the appointment of supervisors for student research projects. Supervisors are generally experienced both as research supervisors and as active researchers. As it is necessary to have a supervisor, it is equally necessary to identify a research topic that falls within the interest of, or is at least within the competence of, staff responsible for research supervision in the department. There have been many examples of potential research students who have proposed very worthwhile topics but have not been able to pursue them because they have not been able to find suitable supervisors. It makes sense, therefore, to find out what topics are of interest to possible supervisors before finalising a research topic. It is often the case that potential supervisors can draw upon their knowledge of current research and help research students identify worthwhile topics for research.

The thrust of institutional research in a particular university or college

Research that is already going on in a subject department or research school is a major source of new research topics. Many departments or schools support research being carried out both by tutors and students, including those working for research degrees. Identifying a research topic that links in with what others in the same department are doing is very helpful in all kinds of ways. Research is an essentially collaborative endeavour and it is extremely encouraging and supportive to be able to talk about a research project and share ideas with others working in the same field. Some departments with a developed research ethos have active 'programmes of research', in which a number of researchers and research students work on different aspects of the same research problem. Checking out what is already being done in a department can lead to the identification of new but related topics. If the proposed research work is highly specialised, most of the equipment necessary to pursue a related topic will already be available.

Commissioned or sponsored research

Experienced researchers often undertake projects into topics that have been identified by others. Research that has been commissioned by industry or local and national organisations and bodies constitutes a substantial proportion of all research activity. Good examples of such research are the surveys or opinion polls carried out by research companies into all kinds of political and other attitudes and opinions. Similarly, most commercial companies, such as those selling washing powders or motor cars, undertake some kind of market research before launching a new product. On a wider scale, the National Foundation for Educational Research is a body that is commissioned by the government and a variety of other agencies to enquire into many aspects of educational provision and practice. In these cases, the general topic is identified by the commissioning body or organisation, and the researchers develop this into a workable research project. This includes developing the research instruments, such as questionnaires, interview schedules or tests, and deciding to whom to address the enquiries. A different kind of example is research into a particular technical process or development, which may be commissioned by, say, a chemical or engineering company. In all these examples, the researchers are employing their research experiences and skills to investigate issues in which they do not have a vested interest. Many departments in institutions of higher education undertake commissioned research and, quite frequently, this forms the basis for research degree work and is used as a research training for students, sometimes as part of partnership schemes between education and industry.

Reporting research outcomes

The reporting of research outcomes is an essential part of the research endeavour and it can be argued that it is one of the crucial characteristics which distinguish research from non-research. It can also be argued that research cannot be said to have been carried out, or was not worth carrying out, unless someone else, other than the researcher, can learn from it. The main purpose of the research report, such as a dissertation or thesis, is to communicate not only the outcomes of the research but also, of equal importance, information about the purposes, methods and techniques underpinning the research. The research report makes the research accessible to others and, by doing so, places the research in the public domain. The accumulated body of research reports in a subject field constitutes, to a large degree, the body of knowledge which is the subject field. Recognising the need to build upon the existing knowledge in a subject field and then contributing to that body of knowledge characterise what may be termed a professional attitude to research. The first aspect of a professional attitude to research is the acceptance that the project needs to be developed in the overt recognition of previous research, and builds on it. Being familiar with previous research, not only in terms of the wide range of methods and strategies that may be of relevance, it is a necessary pre-condition to any form of research. Indeed, it is not only poor research but also a waste of valuable time to pursue questions that have already been answered or to devise strategies or instruments when tried and tested ones are already available. There are no medals for re-inventing the wheel.

The second aspect of the professional research attitude is acceptance of the responsibility to report the outcomes of any research to the subject field. (As may be appreciated, the first aspect is dependent on the second.) There are a number of reasons why this is important, not least that it renders the project open to critical appraisal by others in the field. Such appraisal is not only essential to the further development of the researcher's own understanding but it also makes an important contribution to that of others, including the appraisers. Nevertheless, reporting research to the field can have complications. Some researchers in education and industry, for example, whose work has direct commercial or financial implications, feel that such reporting might leave their work open to exploitation by competitors. However, providing that patenting and other intellectual property rights safeguards are used, this should not be a major problem. Far more important is the value of participating in a shared professional endeavour.

Research reports take a number of different forms and these are determined, to a large extent, by the intended audiences or readership. Research reports to be presented at conferences and printed in conference proceedings may be structured in a different way to those which are to be read in academic or professional journals. Similarly, research reports submitted for academic awards in the form of theses or dissertations may differ from those submitted to a client at the end of a commissioned research project. The format of research reports, therefore, may differ in terms of such matters as length, detail, style of writing, order of content, tables, figures, appendices and so on.

Research reports are meant to be read and, therefore, knowing about the main forms in which research is reported helps to make such reading more efficient. Research reports written by students, apart from showing their interests in and understanding of the topic of their researches, are intended to demonstrate that they have mastered some or all aspects of research methodology. This demonstration of mastery is the main basis on which they are assessed by tutors, supervisors or examiners. Reports produced by experienced researchers, of course, can be expected to be underpinned by a mastery of research methods. The critical reading and appraisal of such research reports by other professionals in the particular field of research is a normal part of the research endeavour.

The four forms of research report that are readily accessible to students, are:

- student research reports;
- research reports in journals;
- research abstracts;
- research indexes.

Student research reports

Students write research reports for a variety of purposes and at various times during their studies at school, college or university. For many students, the culmination of their student research activity and their entry into the career level of professional research is the submission of a research report as a dissertation or thesis in partial or total fulfilment of the requirements for a MPhil or PhD research degree. Some dissertations resulting from the individual research requirements of taught Master's degree courses are at a similarly high level. Although the depth of content of a research project may vary from, for example, that carried out in school or at undergraduate level to that expected of a doctorate, the standard of presentation of a dissertation or thesis needs to be consistently high.

Research journals

The publication of research reports in professional journals is characteristic of most subject fields that engage in advanced work. Most of these journals are published under the aegis of professional bodies or subject associations and, as many of these have a national and international readership, the quality of the content is usually very high.

Many editorial boards use expert 'referees' to review articles or reports submitted for consideration for publication and to judge whether or not they are of a sufficiently high standard to be published. In most cases, professional journals have an adopted 'house style', which covers specifications for presentation in terms of layout, length, form of illustration, use of footnotes, bibliographical referencing system and so on. These specifications and other information about the submission of articles for publication are usually given in the journals.

Research abstracts

Abstracts or summaries of research reports are an important part of the research literature. They are important because they provide brief overviews of what is often extensive and detailed documentation and enable researchers and others to decide which reports are of direct interest to them and are therefore worthy of further reading.

Writing an abstract is a difficult task as it requires the condensation of possibly tens of thousands of words into a few hundred. Depending on the nature of the research, abstracts can usually be expected to outline: the purposes of the research and its contexts; the hypotheses, if any, being tested; the subjects or samples taking part in the research; the research methods adopted; the major conclusions; and the relevance to the field.

Writing abstracts of completed research is an essential part of research practice. Students completing research degrees are required to provide abstracts of their researches, which are included in the dissertations and theses. Similarly, many journals require abstracts to be provided as introductory sections to articles submitted for publication.

Research indexes and databases

Research indexes or databases are categorised listings and summaries of researches in specialist fields and, as such, represent the most direct routes to research information. *Chemical Abstracts*, for example, is reputed to be the largest book in the world with over half a million new entries annually. The entries in many indexes, such as the *Aslib Index to Theses* and the *Allison Research Index of Art and Design*, include abstracts that have been written specifically for them. Research indexes are usually printed as hard copy in book form, but increasingly they are being made available in a computerised form. The computerisation of indexes has not only made information about research more readily accessible, nationally and internationally, but has also made searching the databases available in this form a relatively easy matter. Computerised databases are available either on disk (floppy or CD-ROM) or 'on-line'. The databases on disk are accessible using computers or computer terminals held in the library or department. The periodic updating of these databases is achieved by the publication of new editions of the disks. On-line databases, which may be national or international, may be located anywhere in the world, and are accessed using a telecommunication system through a computer or computer terminal usually held in the library or department. Some of these databases are accessible through the Internet, using a modem, which links a computer to a telephone line, or by a direct telephone line. It is usual for on-line databases to be updated frequently, often on a daily basis, as new information is fed into them. Guidance from a librarian or tutor is usually needed to access on-line databases. Information about researches given in indexes is usually classified into a number of 'fields'. Not all databases use the same format but, in general, one can expect to find the following fields:

1 name(s) of researcher(s);
2 title of project;
3 year of completion;
4 academic qualification, if any, for which the research was submitted, and the awarding body;
5 the duration of the project;
6 the institution in which the research was carried out and the sponsors, if any;
7 details of publications, if any, arising from the research;
8 a brief description of the project in the form of an abstract;
9 key words describing the project to enable identification and retrieval.

Searching indexes and databases

A key feature of databases (see Figure 1) is that they can be 'searched' to provide specific information and, of course, this is much easier and faster with computerised databases than with those published in book form. Most of those published in book form provide cross-referenced keywords and subject lists to assist searches. With computerised databases, depending on the particular database programme that has been

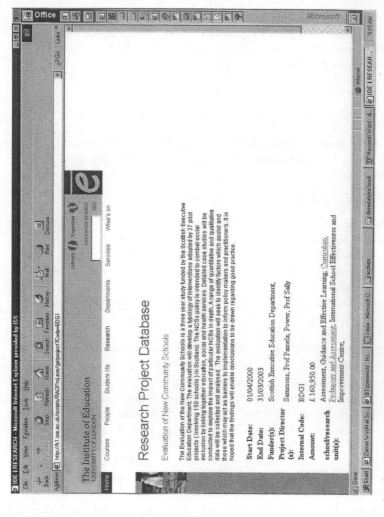

Figure 1 Example of web page showing a database entry

used, searches can be carried out by entering the search requirements in one or more fields and the searches are then carried out automatically. Key words are extremely useful for carrying out general searches on topics of interest and databases can usually be searched by stipulating a number of relevant key words. For example, undertaking a search using the key words INDUSTRIAL + DESIGN + EXPERIMENTAL would find all projects in industrial design that employed an experimental research method. This broad search could be narrowed down by specifying further key words such as:

INDUSTRIAL + DESIGN + EXPERIMENTAL

+ FURNITURE + DISABLED + ERGONOMICS

in order to find experimental industrial design studies which focus on the ergonomics of furniture designed specifically for disabled people.

Preparing a dissertation or thesis

There are a variety of ways in which the products of a study or investigation can be prepared for presentations as a dissertation or thesis. The form in which the material is presented is the vehicle for the communication of ideas and information and, as such, should be recognised as a means rather than an end. Formerly, it was assumed that dissertations and theses would be typewritten, but it is now accepted that they will be word-processed and this book describes appropriate methods for achieving this. Word-processors allow for the choices of typeface and font size similar to those formerly available only to typesetters. This facility enables italics, for example, to be included in the text whereas, when typewritten, the italicising of words, such as in bibliographic referencing, used to be indicated by underlining. Similarly, the fonts in some word-processor programmes include mathematical and other symbols which otherwise require the use of specialised typewriters. The use of word-processing facilities, however, should conform to normal typesetting standards and be directed solely at the clarification of the text. Elaborate options should not be used for mere whimsy or decoration.

It is helpful to be clear about the purposes of academic theses and dissertations as well as to bear in mind the intended readership. It is somewhat salutary to realise that most theses and dissertations have an intended readership of only two or, sometimes, three readers – that is, the external and internal examiners – although, of course, they may be read subsequently by many others. Generally speaking, the purpose of the assessment of any research report submitted for an academic award, whether it is at undergraduate or postgraduate level, is that it is the assessment of the research student's ability to:

- identify a problem;
- analyse the problem;
- carry out appropriate literature and other searches in a methodical way;
- develop a research design employing relevant research methods or strategies;
- select or devise appropriate data-collecting instruments that are valid and reliable;
- implement the design in practice using, if appropriate, samples selected on relevant criteria;

- collate and analyse data using appropriate techniques;
- deduce conclusions on the basis of valid and reliable evidence;
- write up and present a report in accordance with established practices.

It is worth nothing that, although the majority of dissertations and theses are produced in accordance with the requirements of institutions or examination regulations, the copyright is normally vested in the author.

Common patterns of presenting material have been developed over a long period of scholarship so that the contents of research reports can easily be assimilated by readers. For instance, reading is made easier by knowing that, whichever dissertation is being looked at, the bibliography will be found in the same place in the body of the text. Guidance for such preparation of material is plentiful and there are a number of texts that present the reader with a range of information regarding such matters as quoting, bibliographic referencing, table construction and so on. Several of these are included in the 'Further Reading' list at the end of this book.

While such texts are invaluable in explaining the variety of presentational forms acceptable in academic literature, the choice among the alternatives is left to the student writer with the rider that attention must be paid to consistency. This book is intended for students preparing a dissertation or thesis for the first time and for whom making choices from among alternative forms and, at the same time, attempting to be consistent, is often a matter of great concern and frustration. The purpose of this guide is to present a consistent, albeit rigid, pattern which, when strictly followed, will relieve you of much searching of ways and means and so prevent the dissipation of energies that should be properly directed to the content of the study. The practices specified here have been culled from a variety of sources as being the most useful and practical of the acceptable methods.

This guide continues in three parts:

Part I An overview of the task is concerned with the nature, organisation and form of the contents of a dissertation.

Part II Getting your act together – the key processesaims to help you with the key processes for planning, drafting, writing, editing and submitting your dissertation or thesis.

Part III Nuts and bolts – more detail about the main elements is concerned with some of the finer detail of the procedures and practices for producing and presenting a dissertation.

Part I

An overview of the task

Chapter 1

Getting things in the right order

The content of the whole dissertation includes essential preliminary information and relevant support material in addition to the main body of the text. The order of presentation of the contents is normally prescribed along the following lines.

1 Title page
2 Abstract of the research
3 List of contents
4 List of tables
5 List of figures
6 List of appendices
7 Glossary of symbols (for mathematical and scientific researches)
8 Author declarations
9 Acknowledgements (Preface)
10 Text (main body of dissertation)
11 Appendices
12 Bibliography

Note that the actual List of contents itself does not normally come right at the beginning. The Title page and Abstract come first, then the 'List of contents' which presents the headings of the chapters and any sub-headings exactly as they appear in the text, along with page numbers. It should be noted that any pages preceding the List of contents are not normally included in the list.

If your dissertation or thesis contains tables, figures (drawings, screen-dumps, diagrams and so on), and appendices, you will also need to prepare separate pages for List of tables, List of figures and List of appendices showing the exact details of the captions of each table and figure, and the exact titles of each appendix, all with the up-to-date page numbers, so that all of these parts can easily be located in your dissertation by readers.

Naturally, the final versions of your 'Lists' are necessarily done in their final form right at the end of your work on your dissertation, when you know exactly what is on each page. However, it is useful to keep 'running' versions of these lists from quite an early stage, but to pay particular attention to getting the page numbers right as the work develops. Even a minor change in your dissertation can throw the page numbering on each and every one of these lists out!

It is also really important to make sure that your various lists correspond exactly with what they refer to. In other words, use 'copy and paste' in word-processing to ensure that each heading, sub-heading, figure caption, table caption, and appendix title are present in your lists exactly word-for-word as they appear in the dissertation itself.

Chapter 2

Title page

The information to be given on the Title page is normally rigidly prescribed by the degree awarding body. Typically, the required information consists of:

- the full title of the dissertation;
- the full name of the author and, if desired, any qualifications or distinctions held already (which should be included in an abbreviated form);
- the qualification for which the dissertation is being submitted as part of a statement that it is 'submitted in partial fulfilment of the requirements of the award of . . .';
- the degree awarding body;
- the name of the institution in which the research is registered; if different to the degree awarding body, and that of any collaborating institution;
- the month and year of submission;
- the number of volumes comprising the dissertation, if more than one.

The layout of the Title page is centred between the prescribed margins. The vertical centre line is approximately 110 mm from the left-hand edge of the page. An example of a Title page is shown in Figure 2. In the days when dissertations were normally typed, the size of the print was uniform on this page, but nowadays with word-processed work some regulations allow different font sizes for the information. It is best to look at a number of recent successful dissertations or theses to check out local precedents and styles.

AN EMPIRICAL STUDY OF THE PERSONALITY
CHARACTERISTICS OF SOME CHEMISTRY
STUDENTS IN COLLEGES OF FURTHER
EDUCATION

John Brown, BSc, PGCE, Adv.Dip.Ed.

Submitted in partial fulfilment of
the requirements for the degree of
MASTER OF PHILOSOPHY
THE UNIVERSITY OF MIDCHESTER

in collaboration with

WESTCHESTER COLLEGE OF FURTHER
EDUCATION

March 2004

Figure 2 Example of a Title page

Chapter 3

Abstract

There is no second chance to make a good first impression! The Abstract of your dissertation is critically important, and it is well worth drafting this many times and checking and rechecking it. Essentially, your Abstract is an overall summary of the entire work in your dissertation. In fact, although the Abstract comes first in your dissertation, it is the thing you should write *last* as you can write it much more safely when you know exactly where your dissertation led to.

The Abstract summarises what the research question or problem is, and how the work you have done addresses this. Sometimes you will be expected to indicate in your Abstract the nature of your findings or conclusions, but more often the Abstract is much more general, and is intended to whet the reader's appetite enough to want to read your conclusions in due course.

An Abstract of the dissertation is normally required to be bound into each copy of the dissertation and, in addition, it is an occasional requirement for some additional loose copies of the Abstract to be submitted with the dissertation for examination.

The Abstract should not normally exceed about 300 words and be typed single-spaced on one side of A4 paper. The heading of the Abstract, which is additional to the 300 words, should give the name of the author and title of the dissertation in capital letters and the year of submission. The margins should be the same as in the body of the text.

Reducing a dissertation to a mere 300 words is often a difficult and demanding task. However, a well written Abstract demonstrates the capacity of the author to present the main aspects of an often lengthy study in a coherent and economical form. The Abstract, in essence, should provide a brief synopsis of the study by identifying the nature and scope of the work, the major outcomes and the particular contribution it makes to knowledge in the field as shown in the example given in Figure 3.

ABSTRACT

JOY STUART   1989

THE DEVELOPMENT AND ASSESSMENT OF CRITICAL ABILITIES IN ART CRITICISM

The study consisted in the main of a replication of Denise Hickey's (1975) testing of a matrix of the developmental structure of critical abilities, carried out in the USA. The replication study investigated whether Hickey's matrix and assessment were applicable to English education; whether Hickey's research findings and conclusions were valid; and whether replication was an effective method of criticising research methods.

The replication study addressed the problem of the provision of objective measures for critical abilities, and considered whether the development of critical abilities could be associated with intellectual levels and measures of development.

The study was carried out in an English middle school, with a sample of forty subjects, equally divided between subjects aged eleven, and subjects aged thirteen.

The research methodology replicated Hickey's interview format and test procedures. Hickey's measuring instruments provided data for statistical analysis to determine whether the presence of critical abilities could be related to intellectual levels of development. Two diagnostic tests were incorporated into the study to consider the reliability of Hickey's measuring instruments.

The comparability study tended to confirm Hickey's matrix projections, but there were differences between the two pieces of research, which affected the findings and conclusions. The findings were that Hickey's matrix required modification, and that Hickey's assessment procedures were not replaceable. Adaptations to Hickey's matrix were recommended, and an objective measure of critical abilities based on modes of reasoning was devised as an alternative method of determining and assessing the developmental structure of critical abilities. The study also concluded that Hickey's research procedures required revising for a more reliable testing of the matrix and that replication was a sound method of criticising completed research.

The research findings contributed to a fund of knowledge about the development and assessment of critical abilities in relation to intellectual development.

Figure 3 Example of an Abstract

A good Abstract should be comprehensive and succinct.

Dissertations are not normally published, and access to them is invariably limited (though dissertations are often used as the basis for preparing journal articles later). Abstracts of research degree dissertations and theses, however, are frequently published in national research databases. The Abstract, therefore, is important because it can signify whether or not the study is of relevance to a potential reader and, consequently, if it is worthwhile for the reader to seek out the complete work so that it could be read in full.

Chapter 4

Author declarations

A dissertation is produced for the exclusive purpose of the award for which it is submitted. To ensure the safeguarding of this academic matter, it is necessary to include in the dissertation a formal statement that the author has not been registered for any other academic award during the period of study and also to state whether any material included in the dissertation has previously been submitted for any other academic awards. An example of the latter might be the inclusion of material in a PhD dissertation that had previously been part of a MPhil study.

It should be added, however, that it is permissible to publish material arising from a study registered for an academic award prior to the submission of the dissertation. Indeed, where some of the content of a dissertation has already been published during the course of the research work, or is already in the process of publication, the refereeing processes associated with such publication are in themselves taken as significant authorisation of the work itself. Any material published should be referred to in the text and copies of it should be included in the appendices.

As a dissertation is submitted in partial fulfilment of the requirements of an academic award, a statement is included in the Author declarations that identifies the nature of the advanced studies of research programme of which the dissertation is part.

Some universities do not require the Author declarations for a dissertation submitted for a higher degree by research to be bound into the dissertation, but to be made separately on a prescribed form. In such cases, three copies of the form are normally required to be submitted along with the dissertation.

When included in the dissertation itself, Author declarations are placed immediately after the List of appendices. An example of Author declarations is given in Figure 4.

AUTHOR DECLARATIONS

1 During the period of registered study in which this dissertation was prepared the author has not been registered
   for any other academic award or qualification.

2 The material included in this dissertation has not been submitted wholly or in part for any academic award or qualification other than that for which it is now submitted.

3 The programme of advanced study of which this dissertation is part has consisted of:

   (i)   Research Design and Methods course – Years 1 and 2
   (ii)   Participation in Research Colloquia
   (iii) Supervision tutorials
          [All the above were held in the School of Humanities
          and Social Studies, University of Midchester]
   (iv)   Attendance at relevant research conferences.

J. Brown
March, 2004

Figure 4 Example of Author declarations

Chapter 5

Acknowledgements

It is customary to acknowledge any assistance or support that has been given during the research. In general literature, Acknowledgements are often included in a section called the Preface, but in dissertations it is customary to use the heading 'Acknowledgements'.

There is no set pattern for acknowledging help and assistance in the work. In general, however, Acknowledgements should be brief with an avoidance of flowery language, giving recognition without sentimentality.

Acknowledgement of the contributions and assistance of individuals by name should only be made when such assistance has been of a specific kind, which should be briefly indicated. Examples of forms of acknowledgement are given in Figure 5.

Acknowledgements are contained within the normal side margins of the page, but the top and bottom margins may be adjusted depending on the length of the statement, providing those normal margins are not exceeded.

The Acknowledgements page normally follows the Author declarations or, when the Author declarations are not required to be bound into the dissertation, the List of appendices.

. . . and appreciation is due to Dr J. S. Sweeney, Director of Studies, for his continued support and guidance during the research . . .

. . . and to Mr K. Brown, MA, Principal, Westchurch College of Further Education, for advice and assistance in analysing student records . . .

. . . thanks are due to the following heads of colleges and other institutions for cooperation in the testing programme:

- Mr K. Brown, MA, Westchester College of Further Education, Leicester;
- Miss D. Curison, BA, Northfields College, Cardiff;
- Mr E. Dunn, Southlands Community Centre, Birmingham;
- Mrs A. Jones . . . ;

. . . and thanks are due to all the parents and students taking part in the study.

Figure 5 Examples of forms of acknowledgement

Chapter 6

Main body of the dissertation

The order of some of the contents of the text or main body of your dissertation is firmly established while others depend upon the individual nature of a study. A general guide to the order of presentation of material may be seen as following a logical sequence:

1   Introduction
2   Method of approach or attack
3   Presentation and analysis of evidence
4   Summary and conclusions

How this structure is developed in terms of chapters depends on the nature of the research being reported. However, in general, the flow of the dissertation would be expected to incorporate the following elements in more-or-less the following order (though the actual section or chapter titles are usually tailored to the subject content itself, rather than remaining 'generic' as shown below).

Introduction

A relatively concise description and explanation of the purposes and scope of the study and the circumstances that led to its formulation.

Aims of the investigation

A description of the rationale within which the research questions are to be pursued. The general aims and precise objectives of the research are defined. This section often includes a statement of the hypotheses to be examined in the research as well as the assumptions, if any, that underpin the hypotheses.

The context of the investigation

This section normally includes the main survey and critical appraisal of the literature relating to the research topic. In other words, this is your main literature review. It usually starts with a survey of the antecedents of your research, and an account of the development of ideas to which the present research contributes. The theoretical underpinnings of the research are here identified and critically appraised.

Research design

This is your general description of the structure of your research procedures and the methods you adopted. This section includes, as appropriate, your choice or development of data collection instruments or tools, and your rationale for making such choices. It also includes (for example) explanation of your selection of samples, and your time scale for the implementation of the research, and the means by which collected data are to be analysed. Any pilot studies undertaken in developing the research design may be described or reviewed here in full.

Research implementation

This section describes the means and methods by which the research was pursued in practice, including the organisation and administration of the data-gathering strategies. The steps taken to accumulate the necessary evidence to examine and resolve the research questions are systematically and fully described. The resulting data or evidence are presented and analysed in relation to the hypotheses or research questions.

Conclusions

The meaning and significance of the analysis of the evidence in relation to the research questions is described and the conclusions clearly presented. The conclusions are examined in the context of the theoretical positions underpinning the research and their implications for practice considered.

Critical review and reflection

The research is reviewed critically and the strengths and weaknesses of both conception and implementation are identified. This section also presents new questions raised by the research and their potential for future enquiry.

Chapter 7

Appendices

The Appendices section of the dissertation might be thought of as being mainly the repository for the working tools of the investigation and for information that supports the study while not being directly a part of it.

Each dissertation topic requires different kinds of support material, and discretion must be exercised as to the amount of material presented in the Appendices. A simple criterion for the inclusion of material lies in the necessity of that material for the comprehension or illumination of the text.

Special pockets can be made in the back cover of the dissertation binding for bulky test material or material that does not lend itself to being bound in with the normal pages. In some cases it may be necessary to have a special box made to carry the Appendices. In all such cases, an appropriately headed page describing the contents of each appendix is included in the sequence of appendix pages.

Typical Appendices include:

- Data-collecting instruments used during the investigation, such as tests, questionnaires, observation and interview schedules. It is not normally necessary to include standardised test material which is already published or widely known, unless they have been amended in some way.
- Examples showing how the instruments have been used, such as a completed interview schedule, should be included if their inclusion helps the reader to understand the work methods.
- Raw data, particularly if there is a lot of it, rarely finds its way into the main body of the dissertation as it is the analysis and interpretation of data that carries meaning. However, sometimes such

data are a necessary support for the text and should be included as an appendix. Complex or lengthy tables or figures might be included as Appendices either because they would interrupt the flow of the text unnecessarily or because the text includes abstracts or summaries of them. For instance, tables in the text might show the totals or a breakdown of the complete tables that are presented as Appendices.

- It is normally necessary for computer software developed as part of the research to be submitted as part of the dissertation and this could be included as an appendix, or supplied on floppy disk or CD-ROM and contained in a plastic wallet bound into an appendix.

- When the main body of the research results in practical work that is exhibited in some form, it is normally required for a permanent record in a photographic or other form to be submitted with the dissertation. A complete record of such work would constitute an appendix.

- Some dissertations employ a wide range of technical terms with specialised meanings or applications within the context of the research. A glossary of technical terms used in the dissertation, therefore, would be included appropriately as an appendix. A glossary of mathematical or scientific symbols, however, is not presented as an appendix but is sited in the preliminary pages as noted earlier in the List of contents.

- Colloquial language used in response to particularly searching questions in, for instance, an interview, often gives colour to the interpretation of the opinions expressed. Such verbatim responses or transcripts of tape recordings might be appropriately included in the Appendices.

- Long extracts from official documents such as White Papers, Examination Council requirements, speeches and so on, may be included as Appendices when it is necessary to the comprehension of the text for the reader to have them available at first hand.

- Lists of equipment used or observed, lists of schools, firms, laboratories or other institutions visited or reviewed, and other such relevant collations would form Appendices.

Appendices are numbered sequentially with upper case roman numerals (I; II; III; IV). Each appendix should have a heading that states precisely and concisely what the appendix contains, and this detail should be reproduced in the List of appendices near the start of the dissertation, as already noted. Both the appendix number and heading are sometimes expected to be in upper case, but you should check local custom regarding this, as nowadays extended text in upper case is sometimes no longer in favour. If longer than one line, headings should be single-line spaced.

Chapter 8

Bibliography

The Bibliography of your dissertation includes texts, journal articles and all other sources that have been referred to in the body of the dissertation. It does not include peripheral or background reading. The Bibliography is the final selection of your dissertation and is normally located after the appendices, except where the appendices are bound separately, when the Bibliography should be placed at the end of the main body of the dissertation. Bibliographies at the end of chapters are unnecessary.

The examples which follow are fictitious, deliberately written to show *how* to go about writing bibliographic references. Don't try to locate them in your library! Any resemblance to the names or authors or publishers, living or dead, is entirely coincidental!

For references in the form of a real bibliography, please see the 'Further reading' at the end of this book – though that is in fact *not* a bibliography as such, as the sources listed there are not referred to in this book, but are added as further reading. (Don't add further reading to your dissertation, however!)

Bibliographical references

In order to identify a particular text clearly and accurately, it is necessary to have certain minimal reference information. This information primarily consists of:

- the name of the author;
- the year of publication;
- the title of the publication;
- the place of publication;
- the name of the publisher.

Further detail is dependent upon the nature of the publication being referred to. While there is more than one standard way of presenting this bibliographical data, it is important that consistency in referencing is maintained by keeping to one system. The system described here is generally known as the 'Harvard system' and although it appears to be complicated it is remarkably simple to use once the habit of applying it has been acquired. The following examples illustrate the use of capital and lower case letters, italicisation, punctuation marks and layout, all of which have a specific function. In manuscript form or in typescript, underlining is used to indicate typographical *italics*.

Books

The simplest reference form is that for books that have been published as single editions.

Arlington, P. (2003). *Drama Education: Its Philosophy and Psychology.* Minneapolis: Franks and Cobday.

Green, R. (2003). *The Pickleberry Fragment.* Hobsforth: Hobsforth Press.

When books have been published in subsequent editions it is important to specify the edition number as there are often considerable differences between editions. The edition number is shown sometimes in parentheses after the title.

Hill, L. T. (2004). *Business Capitalisation (3rd edition).* Andover, Plymouth: Macdonald and Burger.

Lowenfeld, V. and Brittain, L. (1970). *Creative and Mental Growth (5th edition).* New York: Collier Macmillan.

Collected works

Publications that consist of collections of writings by a number of authors are identified under the names of the editors. Listings, indexes or collections of abstracts are similarly identified by the names of editors. The editors are designated by the abbreviations (ed.) or (eds) after the name.

Pockington, E. W. and Bardell, D. W. (eds). (2004). *Readings in Drama Education*, London: Gunn Baxter.
Wellington, T. D. (ed.). (1999). *Culture and Critical Theory*. Isleworth: Seagull.

References to specific chapters or articles in edited collections are identified under the names of the particular authors and then reference is made to the whole publication as above.

If the date when the specific chapter was originally published differs from that of the collected edition it is necessary to include both dates.

It is standard practice to give the page numbers of articles and, as the whole publication is the primary source of reference, it is the title of the whole publication that is italicised or underlined to indicate italics.

Fairbrother, J. (2000). Personnel Relations. In Weingartner, T. D. (ed.) (2001). *Human Resource Management*. Isleworth: Gannet. 107–135.
Kerrigan, I. (2001). The Art of Curriculum Design in Engineering. In Erlingham, E. W. (ed.). *Confronting Engineering Reform*. Philadelphia: Baker Black and Co. 91–112.

Articles in journals

Articles in journals are always the most difficult to locate so it is essential to have complete bibliographical data. The actual journal in which an article appears is the major reference source and so it is the name of the journal that is italicised. Most learned journals tend to have long titles and so for bibliographic purposes these are reduced to standardised abbreviations. Journals differ in the ways in which the different issues are designated but the most popular form is the attribution of a volume number, which quite often relates to a particular year of publication, and then an issue or part number within a volume. The numbers of the pages on which the article appears are also given.

Timpson, E. B. (2003). The Artist as Critic. *J. Aesth. Meditation*. 7, 1, 50–58.
(In this example the article is in Volume 7, Part 1 of the *Journal of Aesthetic Meditation* on pages 50 to 58).
Flannigan, J. A. (2004). Fragmentation in Restorative Dentistry: The Case for Polyurethane Fillings. *Dentistry Rev*. 28, 2, 317–32.
(Note that page numbers are often abbreviated as in this example).

Unpublished material

Material that has not been published in the senses described above, such as theses or dissertations submitted for academic qualifications or papers read at conferences, is identified by the name and nature of the material as well as the source or location.

> Ewins, R. (2004). *The Butterflies.* Unpublished paper. Second Annual Anderson Lecture. University of Littlchampton.
> Hancock, T. (1999). *Creativity in Gymnastics – A Selective Review.* Unpublished MA thesis, University of Poppleton.

Non-English texts

Texts and other materials written in languages other than English are given the appropriate bibliographical reference in the language of origin but a translation of the title is included in parentheses after the title itself. The parenthesised title is not italicised.

> Galliero, T. W. (2000). *Teoria Estetica* (Aesthetic Theory). Lisboa: Edicao-es 90.

The references for texts written in languages that use characters other than those in the Roman alphabet, such as Russian or Japanese, are given in the full English translation.

Non-authored texts

References are normally identified in the text of the dissertation and listed in the Bibliography under the name of author or authors. However, some texts or other works, such as reference books and journals, do not have a specific author and are not able to be referenced in the standard format. In these cases, the texts are referenced using the title as the identifier, in place of the author's name. When reference is made to a particular issue of a journal, the year of publication is given along with the volume and issue number.

> Howards English Dictionary (3rd edition). (2001). Edinburgh: McTaggart Publishers.
> Hypertalk Beginner's Guide: An Introduction to Scripting (1989). Cupertino, CA: Apple Computer Inc.
> Journal of Interventions and Exchanges 15, 2. (2004). Oxford: Blackbull Publishers.

References in the text of the dissertation to non-authored texts are made similarly, using the title, or the first two or three words of the title, as the identifer, along with the date of publication and page number(s).

> . . . whereas a 'dissertation' has been defined as 'a written thesis, often based on original research, usually required for a higher degree' (Howards English Dictionary, 2001, p. 454).
>
> The Hypertalk words constitute a scripting language (Hypertalk Beginner's Guide, 1989, p. 24).

Non-print media

References to texts or other material available in non-print media follow the same format as print-based publications. The medium and other identifiers are specified within the reference.

> Collings, R. (2002). Jasper Varley's Garden Design Programme 3. (Video-tape). London: ATV.
> Eglington, W. (1995). Effective Mentoring. (Audio Cassette Recording). San Francisco, CA.: Audiotapes.
> Macdonald, R. (Director) (2001). Beautiful Forests. (Film). Broadmoor, UK: Pineforest Studios and Channel 12.

Electronic media

References to material transmitted or available electronically, such as computer games, CD-ROM, the Internet and e-mail, follow the same format as print-based materials but with minor variations. In all cases, specific identifiers should be included in the sequence to show access routes.

Computer programmes

Computer programmes that have been used in the research or have been referred to as data sources need to be identified either as an authored text or by the name of the programme.

> *Consumer Satisfaction Survey Software* (2003). Gloucester: Survey Solutions, plc.

CD-ROM

Material published on CD-ROM, whether reference works or interactive programmes, is referenced in the same form as non-book media.

> MacFarlane, S. (2003). *Introduction to Highway Design.* (CD-ROM). Wellingborough: British Transportation Society.

Internet

References to articles and other material accessible online via FTP (File Transfer Protocol), WWW (World Wide Web), or Telnet Sites must specify the pathway for access. Sites may not be permanent and so the date the site was visited needs to be given. It is of interest to note that the symbol ~ in a reference indicates that the site is a personal site. Keep the address all on one line if possible, and if it must be split do not hyphenate it.

> Frantz, G. D. and McConnell, S. K. (1966). Restriction of Late Cerebral Cortex Progenitors to an Upper Layer Fate. *Neuron*, 17, 1, 55–61. http://www.cell.comneuron/abstract/j0437.html (24 June 1996)
> Li, X. and Crane, N. (1995). *Bibliographic Formats for Citing Electronic Information.* http://www.uvm.edu/~xli/reference/estyles/html (15 July 1996).

E-mail

Articles or other texts sent to subscribers via an e-mail List-serv, including journals published electronically, should indicate the access route and procedure to be followed to gain access. The date the message was received needs to be given.

Worden, S. (1996). *Networking in art and design* (Summary).
Design-Research@mailbase.ac.uk (24 July 1996)
Available e-mail: mailbase@ac.uk. Message: 'Subscribe Design-Research'

Bibliography compilation

When compiling sources of reference into a bibliography the entries
are listed in alphabetical order of the names of the authors. If reference
is made to more than one work by the same author the entries are listed
in chronological order of the dates of publication.

> Smith, A. (1997) . . .
> Smith, A. (2000) . . .
> Smith, A. (2002) . . .

and so on.

In cases where you have cited more than one source by a particular
author in a given year, you need to show which is which, by including
letters in the dates, as follows:

> Smith, A. (2000a) . . .
> Smith, A. (2000b) . . .

and in such cases when you cite their work in your text you need to use
(Smith, 2000a) and so on.

Compiling a bibliography can be a tedious task and it can also be
frustrating when, for example, new references need to be slotted into
a partially compiled bibliography. Some problems can be obviated if,
throughout the research, a record of each reference is kept which is
accurate and complete and in the form in which it will appear in the
bibliography. It is also helpful to have a workable system for organising
the records, such as on index cards that can be sorted and stacked.
Even more helpful is a computer database programme, which can be
added to as necessary, and which, when required, can sort and print
out the entire bibliography ready for inclusion in the dissertation. In
all cases, it is wise not to have the bibliography word-processed in its
final form until after the whole dissertation has been completed.

Bibliographical entries are typed single spaced. In order to make the entries in a Bibliography clearly identified, the second and subsequent lines of each entry are indented, and double spaces are left between entries. The 'Further reading' list at the end of this book is laid out in the form typically expected for a Bibliography.

Part II

Getting your act together – the key processes

Chapter 9

Capturing your research

This book is not essentially about *planning* your research. There are several much more comprehensive sources available to you, going into detail about research methods, drawing up a research proposal, choosing a supervisor, and so on, including several listed in the 'Further reading' at the end of this book. The main aims of *this* book remain helping you to turn your research into a dissertation, and to do it so well that you earn the research-based qualification you are aiming towards.

This Part is essentially about the key *processes* involved in turning your research into a dissertation, whereas the first and last parts of the book are about the bits and pieces which will make up your dissertation itself.

For a start, this chapter on 'Capturing your research' is about making sure that the findings of your research start off on their way to becoming embodied in your dissertation.

Keep files, not piles!

If your research findings are spread around on loose sheets of paper, arranged in piles rather than filed systematically, all it takes is for the piles to get overturned or shuffled and your evidence could be irretrievably disarrayed. It's worth the extra few seconds it takes every now and then to staple related jottings and papers together, and put a title on them, so that they don't become separated. Better still, use a good supply of cardboard wallets or plastic pockets, and write on them enough detail of what's in them to be able to find what you may be looking for, quickly and easily, weeks or months ahead.

Put dates on everything. Make sure that you record the date (and even time) that key results were gathered, the dates where you first analysed the results, the dates where you abandoned particular results, and the dates of absolutely everything you did – whether in the final analysis it could prove to be important or not. It only takes a few seconds to add the date to a piece of paper, but it could be quite impossible to remember when you did something even a few weeks later without that date.

Try to get one little bit 'ready'

Some things you can write long before you start bringing the final form of your dissertation together. In particular, it's useful to write out details of your experimental methodology almost as soon as you've done each part of it, while it's still fresh in your conscious mind. Months later, it would take much longer to write the same account, and it would not be nearly so good.

Don't just *do* your research, *log* it

One of the biggest dangers with research is that you can become so busy *doing* it, that you don't take the time to stop and make notes of what you've done. Writing it all up later may seem an attractive proposition when you're busy pressing on with the research, but in practice it can take much longer to write it up when the important details have faded from your conscious memory. Furthermore, if you train yourself to write things up as you go along, you don't have to carry nearly so much in your memory – you've 'captured' the ideas, processes, details, thoughts, questions, and so on all the way along.

Don't feel, however, that as you log your research that you should be choosing words so carefully that they will survive until the final edition of your dissertation. Trying to write down 'final' commentary or analysis is a daunting task. Remember that the notes you make along the way are just that – notes – and that you can continue to edit and improve them beyond recognition on the way to your final dissertation. But if you hadn't made the notes, it would be a much harder job – all sorts of details, thoughts, ideas, questions could have evaporated away long before you started to put them all into words.

Always have your pen or pencil at the ready – or if you're more comfortable with fingers on keyboard, make sure that you capture your thoughts and ideas on disk really often. Even two hours later, a bright idea which occurred to you could have evaporated away again if you hadn't taken the trouble to put pen to paper or fingers to keyboard.

Start thinking about the wording, as you make notes

At the end of the day, your research is only reckoned to be as good as the words you use to express it. You need in due course to communicate your thoughts, findings, ideas, hypotheses and so on to other people, not least your examiners. So as you practise capturing your research, keep experimenting with the wording. Do your best to say exactly what you mean in language which is quite self-explanatory. At the very least, this will help *you* to make sense of your thoughts and ideas when you revisit them later. At best, you're paving the way to writing your dissertation fluently and convincingly.

Copy everything important

What if there was a fire, and all your data and results went up in smoke? What if someone stole your computer and your floppy disks? Why put yourself under such pressure? For the cost of some photocopying, you can have everything important in more than one place. All the better if it is properly labelled with dates, titles, and so on, so that you can still make sense of it even if the originals have gone for ever in that fire, accident, theft, or whatever.

What if my research gets 'stuck'?

Welcome to the world of *real* research. Research is like that. There are good days, good weeks, but also bad ones. Sometimes you will feel that you're heading up a blind alley, bashing your head against a brick wall, or trying to whisk treacle with your research. Why do you think there are so many metaphors about it? Because it happens to everyone.

There is however one well-tried remedy. Just try something else. Explore a different aspect of your research. Go off on a tangent – even for a short while. It's surprising how often these little diversions turn out to be important – perhaps even more important than the original target where the blockage occurred.

Overall, you need to stick within reason to your carefully planned research programme, but leave yourself freedom to follow-up interesting-looking diversions. Some of these are quite likely to turn out to be more interesting than some of your original research targets – and more worthy of including in your dissertation in due course.

Remember that it's all finite!

You haven't got one million words for your dissertation – nor 100 years to write it all up in. One of the vital research skills you will need to develop is about deciding what *not* to do, what *not* to include, what *not* to read, and so on. In practice, digging *too* deep in research often leads towards blind alleys. It's best to capture your thoughts on what is reasonably close to your research agenda, and resist the temptation to try and make notes of absolutely every little detail which may eventually turn out to have some importance. Many of the details can be ignored, at least until you establish why they may indeed be important. And if they *are* important, you should be able to find them a second time round. So, first time round, concentrate on what seems to be important, and don't go overboard with detail yet.

Don't become a hermit!

Talk to people about your research as you do it. Talk to your supervisor of course. But also talk to any fellow researchers around you. Talk to other human beings too. Explaining what you're trying to do to a complete 'lay person' who has no knowledge at all about your particular subject, can be mind opening for you. The very act of explaining what you're trying to do helps you yourself to put it into perspective, and to work out what's most important. Talking to fellow research students is really beneficial – for you as well as for them. You're all fighting the same battle – to find something worth writing down and analysing, to write it to the standards required, and to be able to defend your ideas in the presence of experts. The more you've argued your case with fellow students, the better you'll become able to argue the same case to your external examiner in due course.

Don't stop reading

Keep reading the literature around your field of study. It changes fast. It can change daily in some areas. At the end of the day (in other words your viva) it is really important that there's nothing relevant and new that you haven't seen – and not only seen, but mentioned in your own work. While it's tempting to spend quite a lot of time on a literature review, then to press on with your own work, it's never safe to leave the literature to itself hoping nothing important will be added to it. Keep doing your web-searches, your scans of the most relevant journals each time an issue comes out, and so on. In any case, your literature 'top-up' activities can feel like a welcome break, now and then, to your own researches.

Chapter 10

Writing it up – getting started, and keeping going

Get started writing, straight away

It's easy to convince yourself 'no point starting writing yet, I've not done enough yet'. However, that road just leads to trouble. There are some things you can start to draft out towards the final content of your dissertation, even quite early in your research. For example, the parts about the research methods you chose to adopt, and why, can be drafted out quite early. You can write a draft account of what you actually did, and why you did it that way, almost before you've finished doing it. You can capture the detail of what you did far more easily while it's still fresh in your mind.

Confront your 'writing avoidance strategies'!

These can manifest themselves in several forms, some of them quite sophisticated. For example:

- 'It's too early to start to write anything up yet'.
- 'I think I'm going to find something really important tomorrow, so I'll not start writing anything up just yet'.
- 'I haven't got anything worth writing up yet – I'll wait till I have'.
- 'The dissertation deadline is a long way away, no point starting writing anything yet'.
- 'I still don't really know what I want to write – I'll need to think about it a while longer'.
- 'I haven't yet cracked the research question I set out to tackle – I'll start writing about it when I've cracked it'.
- 'I can't afford a pen, and I've run out of paper'.

All of the above have one thing in common – they're *excuses* for not starting writing, not *reasons* for not starting writing. In any case, you'll feel better when you've captured even a little of your research thinking on paper. It will be a start towards your dissertation. If you don't start, you'll never finish it. Starting is actually much harder than finishing.

It's much easier to edit and improve, than to start from scratch

You've probably heard the expression 'blank sheet fright'? It's actually quite hard to make the very first written draft of anything. Once that first draft is on paper (or on disk or on screen), it becomes very much easier to *improve* it, to *expand* it, to *develop* it, to *tighten it up*, and gradually to make it worthy to appear in the final version of your dissertation. But you can't do any of these improvements until you've got something to improve, so don't be frightened of the blank page – just get on filling it with Draft 1. There's then plenty of opportunity and time to turn it into that final Draft 37.

Start your literature review as soon as you've started to review the literature

This is something that you can start on really early, on your way to putting together a good dissertation or thesis. Your literature review will be an important part of the final thing. It's much better if the version which your external examiner sees is Draft 37 than Draft 2. The longer you live with your literature review, the better it becomes. It is something to keep editing, adjusting, condensing, expanding, until it is fit for the purpose for your dissertation. Even before you've started on your main research, you're likely to have had your first stab at making sense of what's already been written in the area, and so already have at least some of the material that you will need to refer to in your literature review at the end of your research. Don't leave it all till later. Imagine the satisfaction which comes with 'Well, at least I've made a start on putting together my literature review chapter.' This satisfaction is yours for the taking. This satisfaction helps your confidence to grow. Your confidence helps to assure the success of your work. It's an upward spiral, if you choose it.

Work on several things at once

Don't take the view that each section of your dissertation has to be written, fine-tuned, honed, polished, edited, and finished one by one in turn. It's much less stressful to work on two, three, or more sections alongside each other. This means when you get bored with writing up Section 3, or even stuck stone dead with writing Section 3, you can switch your focus to Section 4 or Section 2 and so on. A change can be as good as a rest – but is much more productive than a rest. Sometimes after working on Section 4 for just half an hour, returning to Section 3 finds the road ahead 'unblocked', and you can proceed smoothly with it.

Don't start writing at the beginning

In several parts of this book, the idea is put forward that the last place to start your dissertation is at the beginning! This is because you can only *really* write a good beginning to your dissertation when you already know exactly where it is going, and where it ended up. Such an introduction will, naturally, be 'lived up to' by what follows. If you write the introduction too early, the chances are that your dissertation will only get some way towards the promise outlined in that introduction. In fact, you can't really write a convincing introduction until you already know what your conclusions have been, or what the answer to your research question turned out to be.

'I've started, so I'll finish!'

Whatever your dissertation does or does not do, it needs to come to a good finish. Don't forget that your dissertation ending is the last thing your external examiner is likely to read before switching into 'judgement' mode, and starting on the task of working out the overall worth of your dissertation. So if you started out with a research question, an answer will be expected here. If you started out to review the state of the art in a field, this is where the conclusions of your review need to come across loud and clear. If you started off on a pathway leading towards a decision between various options, this is where your decision should be clear and unambiguous.

This doesn't mean that your dissertation needs to be the very end of the road in the subject you've addressed. Almost always, there will be further questions that have arisen in the course of the work, and these are often usefully listed towards the end of a dissertation, so that others are able to pick up some of the questions and run with them. You may even do so yourself in the next stage of your own career, if given the opportunity.

The main thing is that your dissertation doesn't 'fizzle out' towards the end. This doesn't lead to good 'last impressions' for your examiners. So it's never too early to start thinking about how in due course you will express your conclusions. In fact, it can be worth drafting out your conclusions even before you've reached them – just for practice, you understand! Also, it's worth ensuring that the last stages of your dissertation don't look as though they've been stitched together under pressure at the last minute. That impression doesn't exactly inspire confidence in your conclusions or decisions.

All this means that it's useful to start paving the way towards expressing your conclusions convincingly, and robustly, quite early on in writing up your dissertation. The earlier you start practising communicating your conclusions, the better they will come across in your final version.

Keep showing people your drafts

It's never too early to get feedback on your early drafts. In fact, it's much *better* to get feedback on your first thoughts, than on your twenty-first thoughts. The earlier you get feedback, the less defensive you're likely to be about what you've done. The less defensive you are, the more likely you are to respond wisely to useful feedback, and develop your writing accordingly.

More importantly, showing people your drafts will help you to find out much more about *who best* will give you useful feedback. There's little value in the feedback 'This all looks very good to me, thank you.' The really useful feedback comes from people who question your ideas now and then, and have suggestions about how you may develop your ideas. These are the people to use again and again – if they're willing – to give you feedback on your draft writings. But you'll need to earn their continued support – what can you do for them in return?

Chapter 11

Organising your files

Earlier on in this part of the book came the suggestion 'keep files, not piles'. In this section, it's computer files that you should be thinking about. Most people heading towards preparing a dissertation keep some or all of their data, results, literature review elements, draft chapters, and so on as word-processing files on computers. The suggestions which follow are based on experience – and particularly experience of getting things wrong. Learn by other people's mistakes, and take the advice which follows.

Keep saving your work – as different files

Suppose you're presently drafting Chapter 3 (long before, of course, you're writing your introduction or your abstract). Save it now as 'chapter 3.1', then save it shortly afterwards as 'chapter 3.2' and so on. Don't just keep pressing 'save'. Before you've finished Chapter 3, you may well get to 'chapter 3.23', but that doesn't matter. What *does* matter is that if you happened to have a really useful idea in version 'chapter 3.17', but which got edited out in 'chapter 3.19', you can still get back to that original bright idea, and bring it back into 'chapter 3.22' and keep it in thereafter. There's no point throwing away what might turn out to be good ideas for the sake of a bit of disk space. When your dissertation has served its purpose, and you've got your qualification as a result of it, you can always delete all the preliminary drafts of your thoughts and ideas, or better still, you can simply copy them to floppy disk or CD-ROM (twice!) and then clear the files from the hard disk of your computer.

Use separate files for separate sections

At the end of the day, you'll need to collect your various chapters and appendices into a single version of your dissertation on computer. Alternatively, you'll need to paginate the separate files so that when printed out they make a complete dissertation. But during the course of production, it's really useful to have all the various bits and pieces as separate files, so that you can continue to work up each part independently until it is ready to take its place in the overall product. Make your filenames *easily* identifiable. You may well end up with dozens of separate files before you start to stitch them together to make up your final dissertation, and it can waste a lot of time if you have to puzzle over *which* file is referred to by *that* filename.

Back your work up

Just as it's important to keep copies of important paper-based evidence of your research, it's vital to back up your electronic records too. What would happen if the computer hard-disk corrupted and lost everything on it? What would happen if your laptop was stolen, along with the box of floppy disks beside it? Go for peace of mind, and have all of your important files in at least three places – for example on a floppy disk at home, on another at college, and on a hard disk somewhere else. If possible, email them to yourself too as attachments, so that if all else fails they'll still be held on a server somewhere in the universe.

Keep records of dates too

Computers automatically save the date at which a file was last saved, but this may not be enough. It can be useful to add by hand at the start or finish of a file the actual date on which you last worked on it (and not using the 'insert field' command which may automatically update the date every time the file is opened). Such precautions can really pay off when you need to go back to a particular file to edit it up, rather than work on the more recent versions which you may have since made but have now decided to reject because the earlier version turned out to be more appropriate for your dissertation.

Don't just work on-screen

Just about anyone who writes using a word-processor will tell you that it's still worth printing out versions now and then, and seeing how they look on paper. There are some editorial matters that can only be noticed on paper, and would not be noticed on-screen. Also, printing out your drafts on paper allows you to pass them on to other people who can give you useful feedback on them, not least regarding spelling, punctuation and grammar. Such things seem to be areas where it is harder to notice mistakes on screen than on paper. The problem with writing on-screen is that you can't so easily see the 'big picture' of your work, and it's dangerously easy to end up repeating yourself, in ways which would come to attention quite quickly when seen on paper.

It's also useful to start keeping printed copies of important files, as you get towards having final versions of separate chapters of your dissertation. It is useful to start carrying these print-outs around with you, and having a red pen to edit and improve your work at times when you can't get to a computer, so that you can quickly make changes to your files next time you are able to work on the machine.

File your files!

If you save, as suggested, just about anything which you may need to return to, you could end up with hundreds of files. It can be helpful to create folders for 'discarded bits', 'current bits', or 'latest versions', or 'still to work on' and so on, so that you still have access to your old files, but they don't fill up your desktop when you open a folder. This also means that if you are just working on a particular part of the overall task, you could simply copy the 'current bits' folder to floppy disk if you wanted to work on a different machine, perhaps at home.

Get to know how to search for a file

Even with the best of intentions, from time to time you'll 'lose' files. They may have been saved to the wrong folder, or have got themselves entirely hidden in some remote corner of the computer's system. If you know what the file was called, you can usually find it quickly by using the 'search' or 'find' options of the computer. When found, immediately save it to where you expected it to have been in the first place, so the problem doesn't arise again.

However, sometimes you will have forgotten what you actually called the file. If you happen to remember the date on which you were writing that file last, you may be able to find it by using search-by-date options. But if you've forgotten what it was called, you may well have also forgotten when you worked on it. Then you're going to need the 'Advanced Search' options on your computer. For example, you can search for a file using the 'containing words' tool. It's then best to narrow down the type of file you're searching for, for example to 'Microsoft Word Documents' (if that was the software you were using). You can then enter words in the same way as you would for an internet search, for example 'results + survey + Lewisham' so that all files containing those three words would be summoned up. If too many files are then identified, you can add more words to your 'search string' until you find the exact file you're looking for. All this takes some time, but not nearly as much time as going round all of the possible files manually, opening them and closing them looking for the missing file.

Chapter 12

Winding yourself up?

This section covers some of the processes you will need to attend to towards the final stages of putting together your dissertation, and preparing for the oral exam or viva which you are likely to have on your work. After all the work needed to put together a dissertation, you might have expected this section to be called 'winding yourself down', but you actually need to be steadily getting thoroughly conversant with everything you've written, ready to answer questions on it all in due course. The time to wind yourself down is *after* your viva, when you know your work has been accepted, and has achieved its main purpose; then winding down is not difficult (though it sometimes feels quite strange to many successful students).

Build in time to change your work

Any external examiner will tell you that far too many dissertations and theses contain abundant evidence that they were put together in a rush at the last minute! All sorts of symptoms can give this away, including:

- spelling mistakes;
- typographical errors;
- punctuation errors;
- grammatical errors;
- mis-matches between figure captions and the 'List of figures' entries;
- mis-matches between contents of the text and the 'Contents' page;
- references included in the text, but not included in the Bibliography;
- references in the Bibliography but no longer in the text (probably having been edited out at some stage);
- pagination irregularities;

- errors in headings and sub-headings (for example something missing between 2.3 and 2.5);
- unfinished sentences;
- inconsistencies between what was proposed in Chapter 3 and what was concluded in Chapter 6.

There is one further symptom of last-minute work which is even more of a giveaway – bibliographical errors – in other words, not getting the references *exactly* right in the bibliography. Elsewhere in this book there is a detailed discussion of how to do this properly (see Chapter 8), but it's not just a matter of knowing how to do it, it boils down to leaving yourself sufficient *time* to devote to doing it properly, and applying a great deal of patience and persistence till you are quite certain that you've got your bibliography exactly right.

Get lots of feedback

Particularly when you're working your way towards the final version of your dissertation, get as many as possible 'fresh pairs of eyes' to look at it, asking people to scribble onto the drafts any comments and suggestions, and particularly to indicate each and every little error they spot – spelling, punctuation, layout, anything! It's really difficult to spot one's own errors, because when you look at your drafts, you tend to see what you *meant* and don't always see what you actually *wrote*.

Don't feel that you have to take notice of every suggestion, however. Work out which are the most important suggestions, and act on them first. Sometimes you will get conflicting suggestions from different people, and you'll need to decide which to act upon, and which to dismiss. Get feedback from different kinds of people. For example, try to find two or three of the following categories of people from whom to seek feedback:

- Fellow research students in research fields similar to your own, who are also going about the task of putting together their dissertations or theses, and who will be in a good position to give you comments about how well your drafts match up to the locally accepted traditions for a dissertation. They may also be able to give you at least some feedback on subject-related issues. In turn, you may be able to offer to reciprocate, and help them with their own drafts.
- Researchers in quite different subject areas. They won't be able to help you with feedback about your subject matter itself, but may

well be willing to say which parts 'read easily' and which parts are more 'dense or difficult', and it could be useful to use this feedback to address the latter areas. Again, you may be able to offer them the same kind of feedback on their drafts.

- Your supervisor, of course. Supervisors are likely to be close enough to your subject area to give you authoritative feedback on the content of your dissertation. They too will have written a dissertation or thesis, and may have useful views on the overall presentation, layout and structure of your work.

- Try to find one or more people who are simply skilled at spotting typographical errors, and mistakes in spelling, grammar and punctuation. If you happen to know a copy editor or proofreader working for a newspaper, magazine or journal, or for book publishers, such people can be ideal. However, almost anyone can find errors of this sort, if asked to look carefully for them, and it's useful to have someone who knows little about your subject area doing this to help you, as they won't be so easily distracted by getting too absorbed with your dissertation to notice the mistakes.

Talk about your work to everyone who will listen!

This is really good practice for your forthcoming viva or oral examination. Get used to the sound of your own voice explaining what you've done, justifying what you've decided, and summarising what you've concluded. Get used to thinking on the spot. Find out which parts of your work you feel really confident about, and also identify those areas where you feel less comfortable – they are going to need some extra practice before your viva.

Practise answering questions on it all

This, of course, is what you'll need to become really confident about, in your forthcoming viva. Write down lists of questions to use for practice. Try to think of just about everything that anyone could possibly ask you about your work. Get other people to help you with this too – ask those who know your subject area to suggest questions about the content of your work, and ask other people to suggest general questions you could be asked.

Then get other people to use your long list of questions, and fire questions quite randomly at you, to give you vital practice for thinking on the spot when you're questioned in your viva. Research students often work in threes and fours, giving each other mock vivas countless times before their real ones come up. They often then report that their *real* vivas were much easier than some of their practice ones, and that the practice had helped them to become much more confident about the real vivas.

Confront what you *don't* know

Naturally, your dissertation is mainly about what you *do* know. It is easy to answer questions at your viva on things you know well. But there will always be at least some questions on things you don't yet know. Sometimes, it is useful to include a section in your dissertation summarising the matters arising from your research, and especially the things which still need to be investigated, perhaps in your own future research, or alternatively by other people who read your work. It is better to have included some 'questions not yet answered' in your dissertation, than to have your external examiner fire exactly these questions at you in your viva.

Expect some quite surprising questions. Sometimes, you could be so close to your own work, that you don't anticipate the sorts of question which will be asked by someone looking at it from a broader perspective.

Don't be thrown by what may seem to you to be obvious questions, or simple questions. Sometimes, external examiners include some very straightforward questions to help to put the candidate at ease in a viva. Sometimes a question may seem quite simple for you to answer – but it may have been asked because the external examiner simply did not know the answer, not being as close to your research as you are. So when you answer, at your viva, what seems to be a simple question, make sure you don't give the impression that the question is far too simple to be important.

Part III

Nuts and bolts – more detail about the main elements

Chapter 13

Page size

The size of paper normally used for dissertations is known as A4 (210 mm × 297 mm) and is used vertically (sometimes referred to as 'portrait'). The paper should be of good quality and with sufficient opacity to ensure the print does not show through. Only one side of the paper is used. Occasionally, an item to be included in either the text or as an appendix, such as a table or diagram, which cannot be reduced, requires a page size larger than A4. While maintaining the normal vertical dimension, the paper may be folded as shown in Figure 6. To avoid being cut during the binding stage of the dissertation, the fold must not be more than 195 mm from the left-hand edge of the paper. Similarly, the folded section edge should not be less than 40 mm from the left-hand edge of the paper to avoid being bound in.

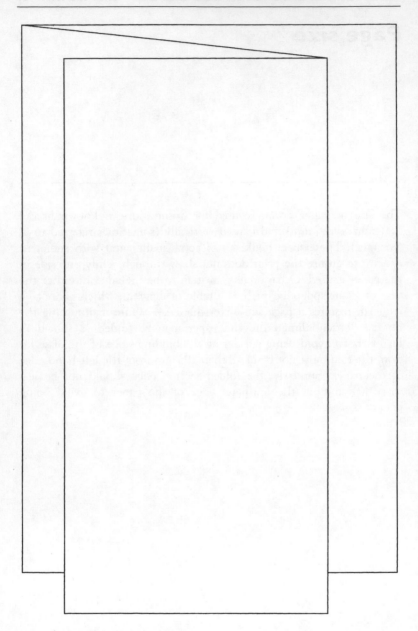

Figure 6 Example of an oversized page

Chapter 14

Page margins

Page margins allow for the sewing and trimming during the binding of the dissertation. The visual appearance of the page is also dependent upon the proportion of the text area to margin area. Margins must be consistent throughout the dissertation. The most appropriate margins for the A4 paper size are:

(i)   Top and right-hand margins   20 mm
(ii) Left-hand margins (the spine of the book)   40 mm
(iii) Bottom margins   40 mm

Pages with exceptions to these margins:

- Title page
- Acknowledgements
- Chapter pages – the first page of each chapter is given a top margin of 40 mm
- Pages that include tables or figures of unusual sizes

Chapter 15

Page numbers

Pages are numbered consecutively throughout the whole of the dissertation. Pages are given arabic numerals. Page numbers are normally placed 20 mm from the bottom of the page and are centred between the margin lines (110 mm from left-hand edge of the paper). However, styles vary in different institutions, so it is worth checking out local practices for page numbering.

The exception to this rule is the title page which, although technically designated page 1, is not actually numbered. Appendices (such as off-prints of articles) that have been previously page-numbered in their publications, are *re-numbered* within the sequence in which they are presented in the dissertation.

As the order of the different sections of the dissertation may be changed while the work and the typing or word-processing of the work progresses, the *final* numbering of the pages should be left until the entire dissertation is assembled. If typing the page numbers in at this stage presents great difficulties, it is sometimes permissible, with the prior agreement of the supervisor, to write the page numbers in ink, provided they are neat and unobtrusive. This concession does not apply normally to research degree theses or dissertations in which page numbers must be typed. To keep the dissertation in order during its assemblage, it can be helpful to number the pages temporarily in pencil.

Chapter 16

Style of writing

The use of a consistent and appropriate style of writing is an important part of the whole research procedure. Thorough and valuable research findings are of little use unless they are clearly and effectively communicated.

The purpose of a dissertation is to present the products of a serious study in a clear, dispassionate manner. It should not be the intention of the writer to be amusing, entertaining or even to persuade the reader to a particular point of view, other than when interpreting the research findings and communicating their meaning to the reader. The main objective is to present the procedures and findings of a systematic enquiry which, for example, might include a hypothesis, the background of ideas from which the hypothesis was derived, the factual data collected, the resultant acceptance or rejection of the hypothesis on the basis of the evidence and an exposition of the consequences of such findings. The emphasis should be on a clear, logical and objective presentation of material with a sharp analysis of the evidence, although this need be neither dull nor pedantic.

It is important to bear in mind the potential readers of the dissertation. As most dissertation topics lie in highly specialised fields, the readers are likely to be experts within those fields. As was noted in the Introduction to this book, the initial readers are likely to be the examiners or assessors of the dissertation. Reading at this level is, of necessity, highly critical and any flaws in reasoning, for instance, or the presentation of unsupported assertions and unqualified assumptions would be quickly noted and, in consequence, the import of the whole study might suffer.

In most fields of research, it is likely that others will wish to attempt to replicate important findings when testing out for themselves hypotheses presented in a dissertation. Such replication is only possible if the description of the research is clear and complete. Ambiguity of any kind not only invalidates the possibility of replication but is often taken to be an indication of imprecision of thought on the part of the writer.

The dissertation can be seen as a logical ordering of a chain of ideas, data, analyses and interpretations. Disordered material reveals little more than that the writer has not understood the relevance of the material being presented. The grouping and regrouping of ideas and data into logical sequences is a major part of the intellectual effort that dissertation writing demands. All writers develop their own methods of organising material, but there is a fairly general pattern. At an early stage a draft outline of the whole work should be drawn up with the expectation that, as the work proceeds, it may undergo frequent revision and extension. The advantage of such an outline, or map of intended or actual development, is that omissions, illogical orderings or questionable emphases can be detected while the work is still in a malleable form. The intention here should be directed towards systematic and disciplined work methods.

Although a completed dissertation or thesis is presented as a co-herent, sequential ordering of aims, procedures and outcomes, it is rarely written by starting on page one and continuing through to the end. It is usual for the constituent parts to be written, refined and rewritten several times. Revising the order in which the parts are to be presented often requires other adjustments to be made. Furthermore, as the introduction is intended to tell the reader what to expect in the dissertation, it is usual for the final draft of the introduction to be written when *all other parts* of the dissertation have been *completed*.

It will be found valuable to give each section a precise heading, showing a clear indication of the content of that section. Indeed, each paragraph should be sufficiently self-contained in terms of ideas as to be similarly labelled, although these would not necessarily be included in the final dissertation. When preparing headings and sub-headings, a consistent grammatical structure and capitalisation should be adhered to. (The box below shows possible numbering and capitalisation, but other *consistent* styles may be appropriate.)

---

4. Controllability
    4.1 Intentions of the Cognitive Dimension
    4.2 Intentions of the Affective Dimension
    4.3 Intentions of the Pragmatic Dimension

The inclusion of non-literal elements, such as formulae, is necessary in many dissertations, particularly in the fields of mathematics and science. In order to identify formulae in sequence, they are designated numerically within the divisions or sub-divisions of the sections of the text in which they occur.

It should be remembered that the purpose of the dissertation is to present a precise and lucid account of an investigation rather than to use the work as a vehicle for the demonstration of masterly rhetoric. A simple, straightforward style of writing is infinitely preferable to the use of long, involved sentences filled with technical jargon. Care should be taken to avoid using a particular term in one sense in one place in the text and in a different sense in others. Any new or unfamiliar terms used in the text should be defined or used in such a way that the meanings are made clear or included in a Glossary. Tenses should be consistent throughout and, as the dissertation is, for the most part, a record of past events, the reportage is carried out in the **past** tense. The logic of this can be clearly seen. The **present** tense is used only when referring the reader to tables or figures in the text or other parts of the dissertation.

As a research report demands a formal rather than colloquial style of writing, the **third** person is normally adhered to throughout. Personal pronouns (I, me, we, you, us) are not normally used. The only exception to this rule is in reporting 'naturalistic' or 'qualitative' research, which may take the form of a diary style of writing. Although the skill of writing in the third person sometimes seems difficult to acquire, most people are able to do it with some perseverance. Attempts to evade this requirement by the use of such ploys as 'The writer observed . . .' or 'One felt that . . .' should be avoided. Spelling mistakes are unacceptable in dissertations as are grammatical errors. The spell check facilities of word-processing packages are invaluable here, though the spell check software may need to be 'taught' many new words during a specialised dissertation.

Spell checking software cannot, of course, help you to sort out the correct usage of 'principal' or 'principle', 'their' or 'there', 'its' and 'it's', 'compliment' or 'complement', 'assess' and 'asses' (plural of 'ass'!), and many other words which are correct spellings but often wrongly used. A dictionary should be used to check any other than simple, straightforward words. Simplified spellings such as 'thro' or 'phone' are not used in dissertations. A thesaurus helps considerably to avoid the repetitious use of phrases. While the dissertation is still at the draft stage it is worthwhile asking lay readers (anyone you can persuade to help you) to check through it for spelling, punctuation and grammatical errors. Better still, if you know anyone with copy-editor experience (for example someone who works for a publisher, newspaper or magazine), their feedback on your draft versions can be invaluable, and can help you to identify and rectify your main weaknesses regarding grammar, spelling and punctuation – we all have these weaknesses!

Authors for whom English is not their first or native language, no matter how fluent they believe themselves to be in the use of English, should always ask a native colloquial English speaker to read through their work before submitting it to a research supervisor. This is not only to ensure that it is grammatically sound but also to tease out, discuss and clarify issues or meanings that might otherwise read as being ambiguous or confused. As writing in a second language is almost always difficult, some institutions permit students to write their dissertations in their own language and then employ a professional translator to produce the work in English. In such cases, care should be taken to ensure that the translator is familiar with the subject field. It is worth noting that where a dissertation is submitted in English, any oral examination of the dissertation is invariably conducted in English.

Chapter 17

Abbreviations

Many institutions, national bodies, academic awards and so on are commonly known by their acronyms or the initials of the full title. While such acronyms or abbreviations are acceptable within the text of the dissertation, the name or title is written out in full the first time it occurs so that it is properly identified.

> . . . within the Codes of Practices of the Quality Assurance Agency for Higher Education for the regulations concerning assessing students. While the QAA expects universities to build their strategies for teaching and learning around these codes . . .

Abbreviations other than those referred to above are not normally employed in the main body of the text. Commonly used abbreviations such as those below may, however, be used in bibliographic references, footnotes, tables, appendices and the bibliography. In the field of information and communications technologies (ICT) equally often referred to as communications and information technologies (CIT), there are now many abbreviations which are widely accepted, some of which are included below. The same applies to the use of symbols and so, for instance, the term 'per cent' would be used in the text whilst the symbol '%' may be used in the tables.

If any other than common abbreviations are used in the dissertation, a key should be provided. This should be placed after the list of appendices, and referred to in advance in the Contents pages.

Common abbreviations and their meanings

anon	anonymous
Bk, Bks	book(s)
c.	circa — about (approximate date, e.g. c. 1623)
CD	compact disk
CD-ROM	compact disk formatted with read-only memory
Chap., Chaps	chapter(s)
col., cols	column(s)
e.g.	*exempli gratia* — for example
edit., edits, edns	edition(s)
ed., eds	editor(s)
email or e-mail	electronic mail
et al.	*et alii* — and others. May be used in the text for subsequent reference to a work with multiple authors after the full reference has first been given, e.g. Witkin *et al.*, 1954
Html or html	hypertext mark-up language (for designing Web pages)
ibid.	*ibidem* — in the same book
i.e.	*id est* — that is (to say)
MS., MSS	manuscript(s)
n., nn.	footnote(s)
n.d.	no date — when the date of publication is not known
n.n.	no name — when either the author or publisher is not known
n.p.	no place — when the location of the publisher is not known
op. cit.	*opere citato* — in the work already quoted
No., Nos.	Number(s)
p., pp.	page(s)
para., paras	paragraph(s)
Pt., Pts	part(s)
RAM	random access memory in computers
rev.	revised, revision
ROM	read-only memory in computers
Sec., Secs	section(s)
trans.	translated by
url	universal (or uniform) resource locator (for identifying websites)
Vol., Vols	volume(s)
vs., vss	verse(s)
WWW	World Wide Web — Internet

Chapter 18

Numbers

When numbers are to be included in the prose of the text, numbers less than twenty, round numbers and numbers at the beginning of sentences are spelled out in full. Fractions are also spelled out unless they form part of a larger number. Numbers in sequence are presented as numerals. Decimal fractions between −1 and 1 require a zero before the decimal point.

One hundred and forty students took part in the experiment, three-quarters of whom were designated as haptic. The responses to Questions 83, 107, 192 and 204 of the questionnaire showed that 121 students considered . . .

The animal's age was $2\frac{3}{4}$ years . . .

. . . the effects of the Revised Code of 1861 were greatly diminished by the end of the nineteenth century.

. . . and of these, 42 people considered that . . .

The freezing point was 0.05°C . . .

The exceptions to this rule are in referring to chapters, tables, figures or appendices in the present dissertation when the designated numerals are used.

As was shown in Chapter 3 and in the observations presented in Appendix IV, the process . . .

Chapter 19

Chapters

Chapters constitute the major way of organising the whole content of a dissertation. Each chapter, however, represents the bringing together of ideas, data or other information relating to a central idea. Although chapters vary in length and complexity, the main issues in each chapter should be clearly evident. It is recommended good practice to include a short summary at the end of each chapter outlining the major points covered and conclusions reached in the chapter. This is not only very helpful to the reader but it also serves to demonstrate the author's grasp of the material. The material within a single chapter may lend itself to being sub-divided into cohesive units. As indicated in the section on style of writing, sub-divisions of chapters should be given headings that clearly describe the content. Sub-headings should be consistent in form and for clarity can be identified by using the decimal system of numbering (4.1; 4.2; 4.3; etc.). Further sub-divisions are numbered by extending the decimals (4.3.1; 4.3.2; 4.3.3.; etc.). Formulae can be numbered by extending the decimals. (4.3.3.2.). However, if there are too many levels of subdivision, such numbering systems become clumsy, especially if successive levels are also left-indented.

The chapter heading should state succinctly the main area of concern of the chapter. Chapters are numbered consecutively throughout the text with arabic numerals. Two line spaces are allowed between the chapter number and the heading which, if longer than one line, is single-line spaced. Both chapter number and heading are capitalised, or presented in a larger font in bold, according to accepted preferences, which vary from one institution to another.

CHAPTER 6

MOTIVATIONAL FACTORS AFFECTING THE
ACHIEVEMENT OF CHEMISTRY STUDENTS

Or

Chapter 6

Motivational factors affecting the achievement of chemistry students

Chapter sub-headings are numbered consistently throughout the chapter and are not capitalised, for example:

6.1   Personality and other background factors

Chapter headings and main sub-headings are included in the List of contents exactly as they appear in the text. This task can usefully be accomplished in most word-processing packages by globally deleting all normal-sized text non-bold, leaving only the main headings, and then turning these into a totally-accurate contents list. Before doing such global operations, however, be careful to save the latest version of the whole work first, (for example as 'version 21.doc', then save it again as 'version 21cont.doc' so that you don't end up deleting some recently-added material when you prepare the material to make up the List of contents.

Chapter 20

References

To a significant extent, the quality of your dissertation will be judged by examiners on the rigour and consistency of your referencing and Bibliography compilation (and of course on your *choices* of references). Comprehensive reference to relevant work of other authors is an essential part of research presentation. Such reference indicates the author's knowledge of the field in which the research is located and is also used to provide an appropriate context for matter arising in the research itself.

References to the work of others need to be made with discretion. It is important that all references are directly relevant and pertinent to the research project and are not included simply to demonstrate the breadth and extent of the author's reading. At any oral examination or viva, you are likely to be questioned on your knowledge and understanding of the work you have referred to, so it is unwise to include references just for the sake of demonstrating wide reading.

References are primarily included as evidence relating to or supporting points, issues, trends and so on, that have been identified by the author. This function should be evident in the way references are made.

There are a number of ways of making specific reference to the work of other writers. It is self-evident that, as full information on every source is included in the Bibliography, it is only necessary to identify each reference to the extent that enables it to be found in the Bibliography.

As a rule it is unnecessary and inappropriate to include any information in the text that can be found elsewhere in the dissertation, as would be the case in the following example: '. . . whilst Sir Cyril Burt pointed out in *Mental and Scholastic Tests*, published in England in 1921, that . . .'. All that is required in the text is the author's surname and the date of publication of the reference. However, there are several ways in which references can be made.

- When the author is being referred to within a sentence construction, only the surname is used and the date of publication is parenthesised.

> While Burt (1921) pointed out that . . .

- References can be made without actually including the author in the construction of the sentence.

> . . . an early attempt at formulating a stage theory (Burt, 1921) may be seen as a precursor to . . .

- When reference is made to more than one author, authors and dates of publication succeed each other in chronological order within the parentheses, and are separated by semi-colons:

> . . . and some attempts at developing stages (Wittgenstein, 1995; Brown, 2002; Lowenfield, 2004) may be seen . . .

- When the flow of the text is uncomfortably interrupted by making references in this way, the reference may be made at the end of the sentence or paragraph providing the direct connection can be recognised.

> . . . although earlier attempts at developing stages did not make this apparent (Burt, 1921). Recently, there . . .

- Occasionally, when a specific point has been made by an author it is necessary to inform the reader of the exact page in the text where the point was made. In this case, the page number follows the data within the parentheses.

> . . . in discussing the role of the imagination, the point made by
> Robinson (1996, p. 114) that . . .

- When reference is made within the text to a work by two authors, the names of both authors are given. If the reference is parenthesised to identify a particular point or quotation, the 'and' is replaced by an ampersand (&). For example, '. . . Hogwarts and Alterio (2003) . . .' would be used within a sentence but '. . . (Hogwarts & Alterio, 2003) . . .' would be used as an identification.
- When the reference is to the work of three or more authors, the names of all the authors are given in the first reference to the work but subsequently only the name of the first author is given along with the abbreviation *et al.* to indicate other authors.

  For example, '. . . Douglas, Newby and Jones (1998) . . .' would be a first reference while subsequent references would be '. . . Douglas *et al.* (1998) . . .' or '. . . (Douglas *et al.*, 1998) . . .' if used as an identification.

- References to organisations or bodies with recognised acronyms or initials are made using the full title for the first reference to the work but subsequently the acronym or initials may be used.

  For example, '. . . Department for Education and Skills (2003) . . .' would be the first reference while subsequent references would be '. . . DfES (2003) . . .'.

Some organisations, such as Unesco, use the acronym as the official name and in such cases the initials are not punctuated with periods or full stops. It is worth looking at recent examples of (successful) dissertations in your subject area (and at your institution) to find out more about the abbreviations and acronyms which are regarded as acceptable, and how these are normally handled.

Chapter 21

Notes

Notes additional to the main body of the text should be avoided whenever possible. It can be argued that if a note is important enough to be added, it is important enough to be included in the main text, perhaps in parentheses. Some examiners are particularly irritated by the use of notes!

However, notes are sometimes encountered in dissertations and can be presented in three ways:

1 as footnotes relating to matters on a particular page; or . . .
2 chapter notes relating to matters in each chapter; or . . .
3 dissertation notes referring to matters throughout the whole main body of the text.

Notes are used for various purposes but, principally, they are intended to provide additional information at particular points without interrupting the main flow of the text. These may be used to illuminate issues raised in the text; to develop or illustrate arguments; to explain particular points in detail; or to give bibliographic references.

However, as indicated above, notes should be avoided unless they are felt to be essential as, more often than not, they defeat their own purpose. Notes tend to make the reading of the dissertation difficult and it is often irritating to the reader to have to leave the flow of the text in order to find and then read the notes. This is particularly the case with chapter or dissertation notes but it also applies even when the notes are on the same page, as with footnotes. Furthermore, the inclusion of the note number in the text, either as a raised number or a parenthesised number, leads to typographic difficulty and, in the case of footnotes, there are problems in judging and balancing the number of lines to be left for the footnotes. However, some word processor programmes make provision for this. When included, all notes are typed single line spaced with a double line space between notes. Notes must be kept within the standard page margins.

Footnotes

Footnotes, when used, are numbered sequentially in Arabic numbers on the page on which they appear. Three line spaces are normally left between the bottom line of the text and the first line of the footnotes.

Chapter notes

Chapter notes, when used, are numbered sequentially in Arabic numbers within each chapter. Chapter notes are placed at the end of the chapter and begin on the page after the last page of text.

Dissertation notes

Dissertation notes, when used, are numbered sequentially in Arabic numbers throughout the main body of the text. Dissertation notes are included as a free-standing section of the dissertation and are located after the final chapter and before the appendices.

Chapter 22

Quotations

It should be accepted as a general principle that direct quotations are to be kept to a minimum as, for the most part, the writer's interpretation of what has been read is more important than merely presenting the reader with a compilation of other people's words. Numerous direct quotations make dull, interrupted reading and often are an indication of the writers' inability to assimilate what they have read into their own thinking. However, occasionally it happens that only an author's exact words will illustrate the point being made or it may be that an author has used words in a particular or personal way. The use of a term such as 'visual thinking' would be a good example of this latter point.

It should go without saying that any quotations included in the text must be absolutely accurate and a clear indication given if any words are left out or any other alterations made. Any unusual or wrong spellings in the original quotations must be included unaltered but identified by being followed immediately by the term [sic]. The term [sic] is always placed in square parentheses to indicate that it has been inserted in the quotation. All quotations must be identified by giving the full reference information including the page number.

There are two ways of quoting:

1 Short quotations of not more than, say, twelve words may be included in the normal flow of the text and are identified by using *single* quotation marks. Note the [sic] in the second example below, where the American spelling of 'behavior' is included in the words inside the quotation marks.

> . . . yet Baird (2003, p. 65) stated that secondary art education 'is ready to reach more people of greater ultimate diversity' and then he described such effort as 'most worthwhile'. This attitude . . .
>
> . . . although the validity of such a notion as that of the 'child behaving as an artist' (Barker, 1995, p. 87) may be questioned. In relation to this point, Barker suggested that the child's 'overt behavior' [sic] may be . . .

Quotations within short quotations included in the flow of the text are identified by double quotation marks.

> . . . while Lorrell and Korngold (1990, p. 154) reported results confirming the hypothesis that competencies 'could be considerably improved by simulating "immediate" reward conditions' . . .

2   Long quotations are *indented* and *single-spaced* so that they are immediately apparent to the reader. Quotation marks are not required. The exact page number must be indicated at the end of the quotation.

> . . . the assertion by Burt (1921) that the child
>
> > . . . is trying, by his pictures, to communicate, or perhaps merely to express, and sometimes only, it would seem, to catalogue, all that he remembers, or all that interests him, in the subject to be drawn (p. 349).
>
> The child, Burt suggested, draws . . .

Quotations within long, indented quotations are identified by single quotation marks.

> An institutional law violation is a violation of the rules of the school, such as . . . 'talk when you're supposed to study', 'not take your seat when the bell rings' (Smith, 1996, p. 743).

Chapter 23

Tables

A table can be considered a complete statistical statement and, in a sense, should be able to exist separate from the text. A table should not need a lengthy explanation on how it is to be interpreted. A well-organised and presented table should be self-explanatory, simple and coherent and bring together a number of related facts to illustrate a single important idea, fact or finding. The purpose of a table is to present statistical data clearly and economically in a way that helps the reader to see relationships, to appreciate meaningfulness or proportions or to assess significances in the data more easily than a prose explanation would be able to do.

A table is always placed after the first reference to it in the text, usually at the end of the paragraph. If it is not possible to fit the table on the same page as the reference, it is placed at the end of the first paragraph on the following page.

Tables should be kept within the normal page margins. Tables that are no longer than one half of the vertical margins are centred on pages of their own. Tables longer than page can be continued on the next page and, in this case, the table and column headings are repeated exactly on the second page. On the rare occasion that a table is too wide to be presented vertically on the page, it may be placed on its side on the page to read from the spine down. In this case, care should be taken to ensure that the margin at the top of the table is the measurement from the left hand margin (40 mm).

It is important that all descriptions of data within a table are accurate and complete although brief. The style should be consistent throughout and, within any one table, the grammatical structure should be the same. Long column headings may be typed broadside to read from the bottom to the top of the page. Abbreviations should be kept to a minimum.

Lines or rules in tables are necessary only insofar as they help to group data in specific ways. Row and column headings are usually separated from the statistics by rules, for instance, as are totals. Side rules are not necessary, though with tables nowadays normally being made using word-processing software, it is often easier to use side rules throughout.

The table heading should state precisely the content of the table. Tables are given arabic numerals, which run sequentially throughout the dissertation. Two spaces are allowed between the table number and the heading, which are both typed in capitals or bold typeface, depending on the particular traditions of the institution. If the heading is longer than one line it is single spaced. Tables are referred to in the text by their allocated numbers. For example, '. . . as shown in Table 9' is used and not '. . . as shown in the following table'.

Table 9 Intercorrelations of background variables (in the diagonal, inter-judge correlations corrected by the Spearman-Brown Formula) and relation to aesthetic judgement

	1	2	3	4	Aesthetic judgement	N
1 Education in art	0.89	0.57	0.42	0.22	0.49**	138
2 Experience in galleries		0.89	0.46	0.36	0.49**	138
3 Art-related hobbies			0.86	0.26	0.21*	126
4 Family attitude toward art				0.88	0.18*	132

* $p < 0.05$; ** $p < 0.01$

(Based on a table quoted in the earlier 1997 edition of this book.)

Tables that are borrowed from another source or publication are classed in the dissertation as figures and are not numbered within the table sequence. In this case, the reference for the source of the table is included immediately below the table.

The List of tables near the beginning of the dissertation presents the headings exactly as they appear on the tables in the text, and is best achieved by using 'copy and paste' in word-processing packages.

Chapter 24

Figures

Not all dissertations need to contain figures, but when used it is important that the visual quality of figures does not let the dissertation down in presentation standard. It should be remembered throughout the dissertation that the major aim is to present data, ideas and information by the most appropriate, economical and efficient means. A diagram or map, for instance, might present a relationship or point of view that would otherwise take up several pages of verbal description. A graph or histogram might demonstrate visually a trend that would otherwise be difficult to present. Examples of art work or other pictorial material, for instance, that was produced or used in the investigation may be necessary to illustrate the text and these may be reproduced photographically, or more often as 'jpeg' files scanned from original pictures or documents, or downloaded from web pages, and then pasted from a computer into a word-processing page.

Included as figures would be maps, diagrams, histograms, graphs, photographs, tables that have been borrowed from another source or publication and any other illustrative material. Colour may be used in figures provided its purpose is to add to the clarity of meaning and is not for the sake of decoration.

Figures always follow, and never precede, the first reference to them in the text, normally at the end of the paragraph in which the reference has been made. If the remaining space on that page does not allow this, the figure should be placed at the end of the first paragraph on the next page.

A figure whose vertical dimension is more than half that of the typed area should be placed on a page by itself. Wherever possible, adjust the reference to your figures so that the figure itself is either already in sight, or will follow on the very next page.

Figure sizes

- Figures should not exceed the normal page margins.
- If the figure is narrower than the margins it is placed centrally between the margins.
- If it is not possible by photographic or other means to reduce a large figure to normal margin size, or if the figure really needs to be larger than the normal page size, it may be bound into the dissertation as a folded sheet, as outlined in the section on Page size (see Chapter 13).
- When two or more figures are being included on the same page, as for instance in photographic reproductions, they should be placed symmetrically either vertically or horizontally.

The figure heading should state precisely what the figure seeks to demonstrate. Headings longer than one line are single spaced. Figures are given arabic numerals which run consecutively throughout the text. Two line spaces are allowed between the figure number and the heading.

In the case of illustrations, such as diagrams, photographs or photographic reproductions, the heading may be placed below the figure on the same line as the figure number. As with tables, figures are referred to in the text by their designated numbers, for example, '. . . as may be seen in Figure 23 . . .'.

The List of figures presents the headings exactly as they appear in the text.

Chapter 25

Typing

Dissertations used to be presented in a typed form, and the accepted styles continue to carry forward this tradition. There are many fonts available to typical word-processing packages, but relatively few are used for dissertations, with 'Times New Roman' (or equivalent) being most typical, and sometimes 'Arial'. It is advisable to look around at past (successful) dissertations at your own institution, and in your own subject area, to find out more about what is considered to be acceptable locally. A 12 point font (12 characters to the inch) is the largest which can be used to ensure a workable number of words per line, and 10 point is normally the smallest suitable size. Sometimes, local regulations will prescribe particular fonts and print sizes.

The visual appearance is of some significance so it is important to check out that the printer being used is in good condition, with plenty of spare toner or ink cartridges available, and that the 'resolution' of the machine gives good clarity on the printed page. It is also important to make sure that the whole of your dissertation can be printed on the same machine, so that all parts will be consistent in appearance.

The same font type and size should be used for all the body text throughout the dissertation, though follow local precedents regarding using **bold** text for headings, and perhaps larger fonts for main headings.

Word-processing packages allow a range of line spacing options, but it is normal for dissertations to be printed double-line spaced, though with some machines one and a half-line spaces are acceptable. A further space should be allowed between paragraphs. The only occasions when single-line spacing is normally used are:

1   The Abstract
2   Chapter, table, figure or appendix headings
3   Long, direct quotations
4   Bibliographical entries

Word-processors with automatic spacing should be 'left justified'. Because of the limited number of words allowed by the dissertation margins, type that is right-and-left (or 'fully') justified leaves uneven, awkward spaces between words, and makes reading difficult.

If you are already a competent typist, you may find it useful to prepare your dissertation yourself. This has the advantage that you can retain full control of some of the more difficult aspects, for example the inclusion of equations, tables, and figures in your dissertation. Even if you are not particularly skilled at the word-processor keyboard, it can be useful to make your own draft versions, before passing the near-final version to a skilled typist. Despite the cost, for many researchers it is more than worthwhile to have the final version(s) of a dissertation typed professionally. Employing a reliable and competent typist can save a great deal of anguish and frustration, particularly when working to a deadline. Before finalising an arrangement for typing, it is advisable to ask the typist to type a few pages to ensure that the accuracy and quality are acceptable, and to check that the typist knows the locally accepted standards and formats for the production and presentation of dissertations.

At least four printed copies of a dissertation are normally required. Good quality photocopies are now accepted by most degree awarding bodies, which can be useful if certain additions need to be made by hand to a printed master-copy, for example numbering of appendix pages. It can also be less time-consuming and cheaper to make photocopies of word processed dissertations than to produce additional print-outs from the word processor.

If you are having your final version produced by a professional typist, both of you can save time and trouble as follows:

• The final draft of the manuscript should be clearly written or, preferably, draft-typed. No matter how poorly typed it may be in the first place, typescript is much easier for a typist to work from than manuscript, or better still, supplied already on disk in a suitable word-processor format, so that it can be edited on-screen rather than completely re-typed.

- If you're employing a typist who does not know intimately the layout requirements for your dissertation, make sure that you supply exact page mock-ups, or provide an example of a good past dissertation as an example of page layout and structure.
- Be realistic about how long it will take for the typist to carry out the work. Work backwards from the deadline date for the submission of the dissertation.
- Keeping in close touch with the typist, particularly in the early stages, facilitates checking the typing quality, layout, spelling and so on.

When the dissertation is in its final typed form, it is your responsibility as the author to proof-read the work. Proof-reading can be tedious, particularly when you have lived with material for a long time and often feel that you know it word for word. However, proof-reading is a vital part of dissertation preparation and you should try to detach yourself from your work, almost to the point of imagining that it has been written by someone else. If possible, make every effort to get someone else to proof-read the work as well, several people if you can. A fresh pair of eyes will often pick up points that would otherwise go unnoticed. The proof-reading stage is not simply to check the accuracy of the manuscript regarding spelling and punctuation but it also provides a final opportunity to check for consistency, logic and the appropriateness of the organisation of your ideas and data. You need to be quite ruthless, even at this late stage, in making revisions or amendments when they are necessary. It is worth remembering that the next readers are likely to be your examiners.

Chapter 26

Binding

Dissertations are normally required to be bound in one form or another prior to submission for examination, and in due course to be bound in a prescribed format after being accepted (and after any changes which are suggested or imposed by the examiners are made). Some degree-awarding institutions allow dissertations to be submitted in a 'semi-permanent' binding, which could range from a glued spine form within a soft cover, to a loose-leaf form (provided they are securely held together such as in a spring-back binder). You may not be required to have your dissertation bound in hard covers until after acceptance.

Bindings should be of a fixed type so that pages cannot be removed or replaced. The front and back boards need to be of sufficient thickness to support the weight of the dissertation when it is standing upright. If the dissertation as a single volume would exceed 70 mm thickness, it is normal for it to be bound as two or more volumes. Dissertations may be required to be covered in cloth or linen which should be of a colour and quality approved by the institution.

The title of the dissertation, the name and initials of the author, the qualification and the year of submission must normally appear on the *front* board of the dissertation. A normal requirement is that the title should be in 'at least 24pt print' but, with approval, a smaller print size may be used if the title is too long for this size to be visually acceptable. The name and initials of the author, the qualification and the year of submission must be tooled on the *spine*. If the dissertation comprises more than one volume, the volume number must also be placed on the spine. Lettering on the spine is normally horizontal when the dissertation is standing upright but may be placed along the spine if the dissertation is too thin to carry horizontal letters. In this case, the letters must be upright when the dissertation is lying on its back. Unless an institution has specific regulations, the layout for the lettering on a dissertation cover should be as shown in Figure 7.

M. Phil	**AN EMPIRICAL STUDY OF THE PERSONALITY CHARACTERISTICS OF SOME CHEMISTRY STUDENTS IN COLLEGES OF FURTHER EDUCATION**
J. BROWN	**J. BROWN** **MASTER OF PHILOSOPHY**
2005	**UNIVERSITY OF MIDCHESTER** **2005**

Figure 7 Example of a binding layout

Lettering is normally tooled in gold.

Preferably, dissertations should be bound by a commercial book-binder experienced in binding academic work. Supervisors should be asked to recommend suitable bookbinders, or your institutional library will have staff who are able to advise. The bookbinder should be consulted at an early stage if it is intended to include unusual material such as folded pages or appendix material which needs to have a pocket made in the rear cover.

If the submission includes a substantial amount of bulky non-textual material, such as records of visual material or other practical work sub-mitted for assessment, that cannot be accommodated in a pocket in the rear cover of the dissertation, it may be necessary to have a suitable case made. Whenever possible, the size of the front cover of the case should be the same as the dissertation but, if the material dictates it, it may be necessary for it to be larger. In all cases, the bookbinder should be asked to make a case that matches the dissertation binding, including the lettering. In these cases, the word 'Appendices' should be included on the spine and front cover.

Chapter 27

Instructions for typists

These instructions may be copied (or amended to fit in with local practices in your own institution) and given to anyone producing the final version of your dissertation.

1 **Paper size**   A4

2 **Margins**   Top and right hand margin   20 mm
Left hand margin   40 mm
Bottom margin   40 mm
Exception – the first page of each chapter has a top margin of 40 mm.

3 **Page numbers**   Page numbers are to be 20 mm from the bottom edge of the page and central between the margins (110 mm from the left hand edge of the page).

4 **Type**   Typographical style must be consistent throughout the whole dissertation.
4.1 Normal lines of text are typed double-spaced with *three* line spaces between paragraphs.
4.2 Single line spaces are used in:
4.2.1 Long quotations, which are also indented four characters from each margin.
4.2.2 Chapter, table, figure and appendix headings when longer than one line.
4.2.3 The Abstract.

4.2.4 Bibliographical entries, which are also inset four characters on the second and subsequent lines. *Double-line* spaces are used between entries in the Bibliography.

4.3 Capital letters or bold print are used throughout for chapter, table, figure and appendix headings.

Further reading

Allison, B., O'Sullivan, T., Owen, A., Rice, J. Rothwell, A. and Saunders, C. (1996) *Research Skills for Students*. London: Kogan Page.

Bell, J. (1999) *Doing your Research Project*: 3rd edition. Buckingham: Open University Press.

Bell, J. and Opie, C. (2002) *Learning from Research: Getting more from your data*. Buckingham: Open University Press.

Bellquist, J. E. (1993) *A Guide to Grammar and Usage for Psychology and Related Fields*. Hove: Lawrence Erlbaum Associates Ltd.

Blaxter, L., Hughes, C. and Tight, M. (2001) *How to Research:* 2nd edition. Buckingham: Open University Press.

Bolker, J. (1998) *Writing Your Dissertation in Fifteen Minutes a Day*. Bellingham, Washington: Wise Owl Books.

Carroll, J. (2002) *A Handbook for Deterring Plagiarism in Higher Education*. Oxford: Oxford Centre for Staff and Learning Development, Oxford Brookes University.

Creme, P. and Lea, M. R. (1997) *Writing at University*. Buckingham: Open University Press.

Cryer, P. (2000) *The Research Student's Guide to Success:* 2nd edition. Buckingham: Open University Press.

Davis, G. B. and Parker, A. C. (1997) *Writing the Doctoral Dissertation: a Systematic Approach*. Hauppauge, Long Island, USA: Barron's.

Dunleavy, P. (2003) *Authoring a PhD: How to Plan, Draft, Write and Finish a Doctoral Thesis or Dissertation*. Basingstoke: Palgrave Macmillan.

Li, X. and Crane, N. (1996) *Electronic Style: A Guide to Citing Electronic Information* (rev. edit.). Westport, CT: Mecklermedia.

Murray, R. (2002) *How to Write a Thesis*. Buckingham: Open University Press.

Phillips, E. M. and Pugh, D. S. (2000) *How to Get a PhD:* 3rd edition. Buckingham: Open University Press.

Swetnam, D. (2000) *Writing your Dissertation*. Oxford: How To Books.

Watson, G. (1987) *Writing a Thesis: A Guide to Long Essays and Dissertations*. Harlow: Longman.

White, B. (2000) *Dissertation Skills*. London: Continuum International Publishing Group.

Wisker. G. (2001) *The Postgraduate Research Handbook: Succeed with Your MA, MPhil, EdD and PhD* (Palgrave Study Guides). Basingstoke: Palgrave Macmillan.

Index